CARDIFF
TO
PONTYPRIDD

Vic Mitchell and Keith Smith

MP *Middleton Press*

Published May 2011

ISBN 978 1 906008 95 6

© Middleton Press, 2011

Design Deborah Esher

Published by
> *Middleton Press*
> *Easebourne Lane*
> *Midhurst*
> *West Sussex*
> *GU29 9AZ*

Tel: 01730 813169
Fax: 01730 812601
Email: info@middletonpress.co.uk
www.middletonpress.co.uk

Printed in the United Kingdom by Henry Ling Limited, at the Dorset Press, Dorchester, DT1 1HD

CONTENTS

INDEX

Ia.   GWR map for 1947. Stops north of Coryton are not shown, as passenger services ceased in 1931. The terminus had been near Treforest and was called Rhydyfelin Halt Low Level. Trains north from Caerphilly did not enter Pontypridd station until 1922, terminating south of it at Tram Road Halt. This then closed and so it is not shown either. Neither are the stations on the line bypassing Pontypridd; these can be found in pictures 88 to 92 and were on the Barry Railway.

GEOGRAPHICAL SETTING

The ancient settlement of Cardiff is at an early crossing point of the River Taff and it developed as a commercial centre, port and capital city. At the eastern end of the Vale of Glamorgan, it became challenged as a location for coal export by nearby Penarth and later by Barry Docks.

The coal basin is deep underground at its centre, but its periphery is surrounded by a limestone ridge. A gap in it accommodates the River Taff and coal was dug or mined in adits near the limestone. It is still obtained in open cast pits at the northern edge, but the deep pits have closed.

The Taff gap gave rise to a famous well and attracted more than one railway to make an easy path through the ridge. Between the coal and the limestone is a thin deposit of red sandstone, much sought after for prestigious buildings. All the lines were built in the county of Glamorganshire, but this ceased to exist administratively in 1974, upon local government reorganisation.

The maps are to the scale of 25ins to 1mile, with north at the top unless otherwise indicated. Welsh spelling and hyphenation has varied over the years, therefore we have generally used the form of the period.

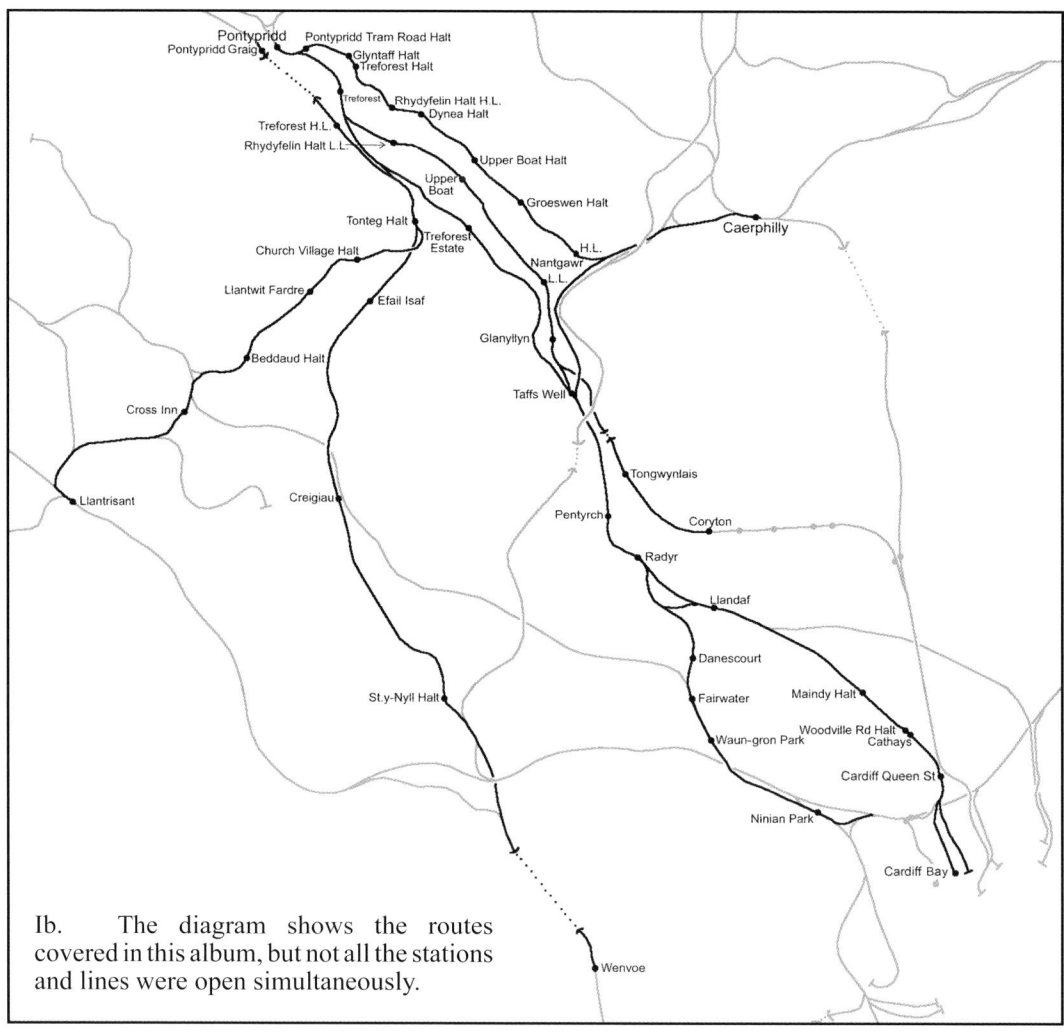

Ib.   The diagram shows the routes covered in this album, but not all the stations and lines were open simultaneously.

HISTORICAL BACKGROUND

The Taff Vale Railway's route was authorised under an Act of 21st June 1836 and it was opened from Cardiff to Abercynon (north of Pontypridd) on 9th October 1840. It was extended to Merthyr in 1841 and its engineer was I.K.Brunel, who specified standard gauge. However, he used broad gauge track for the South Wales Railway, which opened between Chepstow and Swansea in 1850. The TVR was regarded as a local line linking the collieries with the docks of Lord Bute and would have no relationship with the main line on the coast. The TVR route was doubled from 1857 onwards.

The Rhymney Railway had the same purpose and opened in 1858, but joined the TVR near Taffs Well. Its own direct route to Cardiff from Caerphilly followed in 1871, after the completion of a long tunnel.

The SWR became part of the Great Western Railway in 1863 and it ran standard gauge trains from 1872. The Penarth Harbour, Dock & Railway opened a mineral line south from Radyr to the harbour in 1859, this giving a fresh access to ships for coal loading.

The Barry Dock & Railways Company created a third loading point for colliers, when its route through Wenvoe to the Taff Vale opened in 1889. It ran via Creigiau, where it passed over the Llantrisant & Taff Vale Railway of 1886. This mineral line linked the area north of Llantrisant with Penarth Docks and became part of the TVR in 1889. The BD&R became simply the Barry Railway in 1891 and it diverged north of the GWR main line to connect with various valley lines, notably the TVR south of Treforest. These two railways were absorbed by the GWR in 1922.

The Pontypridd, Caerphilly & Newport Railway operated in those districts from 1884, the route carrying passengers non-stop between the first two places from 28th December 1887. The northern terminus was at Tram Road Halt until 1922. The line became part of the Alexandra (Newport & South Wales) Docks & Railway in 1897 and a series of halts was opened on 1st September 1904.

The Cardiff Railway reached Treforest in 1909 and a passenger service ran between Cardiff, Coryton and Rhydyfelin Halt from 1st March 1911. It ceased north of Coryton on 20th July 1931. Both companies were absorbed into the GWR in 1922.

The GWR formed the Western Region of British Railways upon nationalisation in 1948 and passenger services to the Taff Vale from Llantrisant were lost in 1952, from Caerphilly to Pontypridd in 1956 and from Barry, Wenvoe and Ely in 1962. Details of these and withdrawals of freight services are given in the captions. Most services were diesel operated from 13th January 1958.

The route between Cardiff Central and Radyr via Ninian Park had its first regular passenger services from 4th October 1987.

Privatisation in 1996 resulted in South Wales & West providing services ("South" was dropped in 1998). However, after reorganisation in 2001, Wales & Borders became the franchisee and Arriva Trains Wales took over in December 2003.

The former TVR main line and its 1841 branch from Pontypridd to the Rhondda Valley are still both busy.

ACKNOWLEDGEMENTS

We are very grateful for the assistance received from many of those mentioned in the credits also to B.Bennett, A.R.Carder, R.Caston, G.Croughton, S.C.Jenkins, M.A.N.Johnston, P.J.Kelley, N.Langridge, B.Lewis, D.T.Rowe, Mr D. and Dr S.Salter, G.T.V.Stacey, S.Vincent T.Walsh and in particular, our always supportive wives, Barbara Mitchell and Janet Smith.

Gradient Profile.

II.	The 1954 map at 1ins to 1 mile has the main line from Newport and the main road (A48) across the lower right corner of the right page. Queen Street station is close to the road and the ex-RR line runs north, while our route is marked diagonally to Radyr, where it turns north. Cardiff is lower right on the right page and Pontypridd is at the top of the left page.

PASSENGER SERVICES

Cardiff to Pontypridd

The table below indicates the train frequency over more than a century:

	Weekdays	Sundays
1841	4	0
1850	3	2
1869	4	2
1895	15	2
1921	26	4
1950	37	9

Since the advent of dieselisation in the late 1950s, a regular interval (clock face) service has been provided, with most trains originating at Penarth or Barry. Since 2005, many have started at Bridgend, running via Barry.

Taff Vale from Wenvoe

The service between Barry and Pontypridd stood at three trains on weekdays and two on Sundays for its entire 66 years. However, trains ceased to call at Wenvoe on Sundays from 1930, but in the Summer there were extras from various valleys to Barry Island, for recreational purposes. They did not run in wartime. In the early years, they ran north to and from Trehafod.

Taff Vale from Llantrisant

There were three trains on weekdays in 1875, six in 1899, eleven in 1911, ten in 1930 and only four in 1951, the last full year. We have found no regular Sunday services.

Taff Vale from Caerphilly

The Pontypridd, Caerphilly & Newport Railway provided the first service, this beginning on 28th December 1887 and it offered three trains each way daily between the towns mentioned. It was taken over by the Alexandra Docks & Railway Company in 1897. RR trains called at Machen from 1908 when three halts were opened and its service of nine railmotors began between there and Caerphilly. The GWR then ran the four trains between Newport and Pontypridd.

There were severe reductions during World War I, but recovery brought five trains in 1922, when the GWR took over the AD&R. It then extended the service from Tram Road Halt to its own station, Pontypridd Central. The 1912 timetable extract does not reveal that Tram Road was the end of the journey! In 1930, 14 trips were on offer, this diminishing to nine by 1955.

Taff Vale from Coryton

The initial timetable had eleven weekday and five Sunday trains between Cardiff (Rhymney) and Rhydyfelin Low Level Halt. There were still ten and four in 1918, but the 1920s saw several journeys cut back to Whitchurch and Sunday trains vanished. They were all operated by steam railmotors until about 1920. There were nine in 1930, the last complete year.

Taff Vale from Ninian Park

Only occasional trains for football supporters and other pleasure traffic visited the halt at Ninian Park. After the route opened as the "City Line" in October 1987, it had a basic half-hourly service, weekdays only, between Coryton and Taffs Well. It has subsequently only run between Cardiff Central and Radyr.

Secretary, Edwd. Kenway, Cardiff.						**TAFF VALE AND ABERDARE.**							Engineer, E. Highton.	
Mls.	**Down.**	mail mixd	mixd	mixd	SUNDAYS. mixd	mixd	Fares from Merthyr.	**Up.**	mail mixd	mixd	mixd	SUNDAYS. mail mixd	Fares From Cardiff.	
		morn aft	aft	aft	morn	aft	1 clss 2 clss 3 clss s. d. s. d. s. d.		morn	aft	aft	morn aft	1 clss 2 clss 3 cls s. d. s. d. s. d.	
—	**Merthyr** dep.	7 45 1 10	5 40	8 15	4 10			**Cardiff Dock.**	8 45	12 45	5 15	9 15 3 45		
2¼	Troedyrhiew....	7 54 1 19	5 49	8 24	4 19	0 6 0 4 0 3	**Cardiff**	9 0	1 0	5 30	9 30 4 0	.. .. ..	
7¼	Incline Top	8 15 1 40	6 10	8 45	4 40	1 6 1 0 0 8	Llandaff........	9 9	1 10	5 40	9 39 4 10	0 8 0 4 0 3	
8	Aberdare Junc. d.	8 25 1 50	6 20	8 55	4 50	1 6 1 0 0 8	Pentyrch	9 16	1 18	5 48	9 46 4 18	1 0 0 8 0 6	
11¼	Newbridge......	8 35 1 59	6 30	9 5	5 0	2 0 2 6 1 0	Taff's Well	9 21	1 24	5 54	9 51 4 24	1 3 1 0 0 8	
12¼	Treforest	8 41 2 5	6 36	9 11	5 6	2 0 2 6 1 0	Treforest	9 34	1 38	6 8	10 4 4 38	2 0 1 6 1 0	
16¼	Taff's Well	8 55 2 18	6 50	9 25	5 20	2 9 2 0 1 4	Newbridge......	9 39	1 43	6 13	10 9 4 43	2 0 1 6 1 0	
18	Pentyrch	9 1 2 23	6 56	9 31	5 26	3 0 2 4 1 6	Aberdare Junc...	9 50	1 55	6 25	10 20 4 55	2 8 2 0 1 4	
20¼	Llandaff........	9 9 2 30	7 4	9 39	5 34	3 6 2 8 1 9	Incline Top	10 0	2 5	6 35	10 30 5 5	2 8 2 0 1 4	
23¼	**Cardiff**....arr.	9 20 2 40	7 15	9 50	5 45	4 0 3 0 2 0	Troedyrhiew....	10 20	2 25	6 55	10 50 5 25	3 6 2 9 1 9	
24¼	**Cardiff Dk.** „	9 30 2 50	7 25	10 0	5 55	.. .. ..	**Merthyr**..arr	10 30	2 35	7 5	11 0 5 35	4 0 3 0 2 0	
16¼	Mill Street.. dep.	7 30 1 0	5 30	8 5	4 0		Aberdare Junc...	9 55	2 0	6 30	10 25 5 0	.. .. ..	
15¼	Aberdare .. „	7 40 1 10	5 40	8 15	4 10	2 0 1 6 1 0	Mountain Ash ..	10 11	2 16	6 46	10 41 5 14	3 4 2 6 1 8	
14¼	Treaman	7 45 1 14	5 44	8 19	4 14	2 0 1 6 1 0	Aberaman......	10 20	2 25	6 55	10 50 5 22	4 0 3 0 2 0	
13¼	Aberaman	7 50 1 17	5 47	8 22	4 17	2 0 1 6 1 0	Treaman........	10 24	2 29	6 59	10 54 5 25	4 0 3 0 2 0	
12	Mountain Ash ..	7 58 1 25	5 55	8 30	4 25	2 0 1 6 1 0	Aberdare....arr.	10 30	2 35	7 5	11 0 5 30	4 0 3 0 2 0	
18	Aberdare Junc ..	8 15 1 40	6 10	8 45	4 40	.. .. ..	Mill Street.... „	10 40	2 46	7 15	11 10 5 45	.. .. ..	

March 1850

June 1869

* Adjoins Penarth Dock Station.　† Adjoins Main Line Station.　**b** Except Saturdays to and from Clarence Road.

June 1897

CARDIFF and RHYDYFELIN (Motor Cars).—Cardiff.

Gen. Man., C. S. Denniss.　　Chief Eng., H. S. C. Ree.　　Traffic Supt., W. J. Holloway.　　Sec., H. A. Roberts.

¶ "Halts" at Heath and Rhubina, between Cardiff and Whitchurch; Coryton, between Whitchurch and Tongwynlais: and Nantgarw, between Glanllyn and Upper Boat.

October 1912

PONTYPRIDD and CAERPHILLY (Motor Cars).—Alexandra, Newport, and South Wales

¶ "Halts" at Glyntaff, Treforest, Rhydyfelin, Dynea, Upper Boat, Groeswen, and Nantgarw, between Pontypridd and Caerphilly.

October 1912

Map labels: MORGANSHIRE CANAL, Towing Path, West Yard (Taff Vale Ry.), Stone, Cardiff Exchange, L.B., Bute Street, S.P., Dock Sta., Saw Mills, Cr., Warehouse, South Wales & Liverpool Steam Packet Warehouses, C.D., Dock Chambers, Bank, Docks Lane, Custom House, Warehouse, Cr., Coal Staith, M.P³, Coal Staith, Engine W, Chapel, Caisson M P³, Church, COLLINGDON, COLLINGDON ROAD

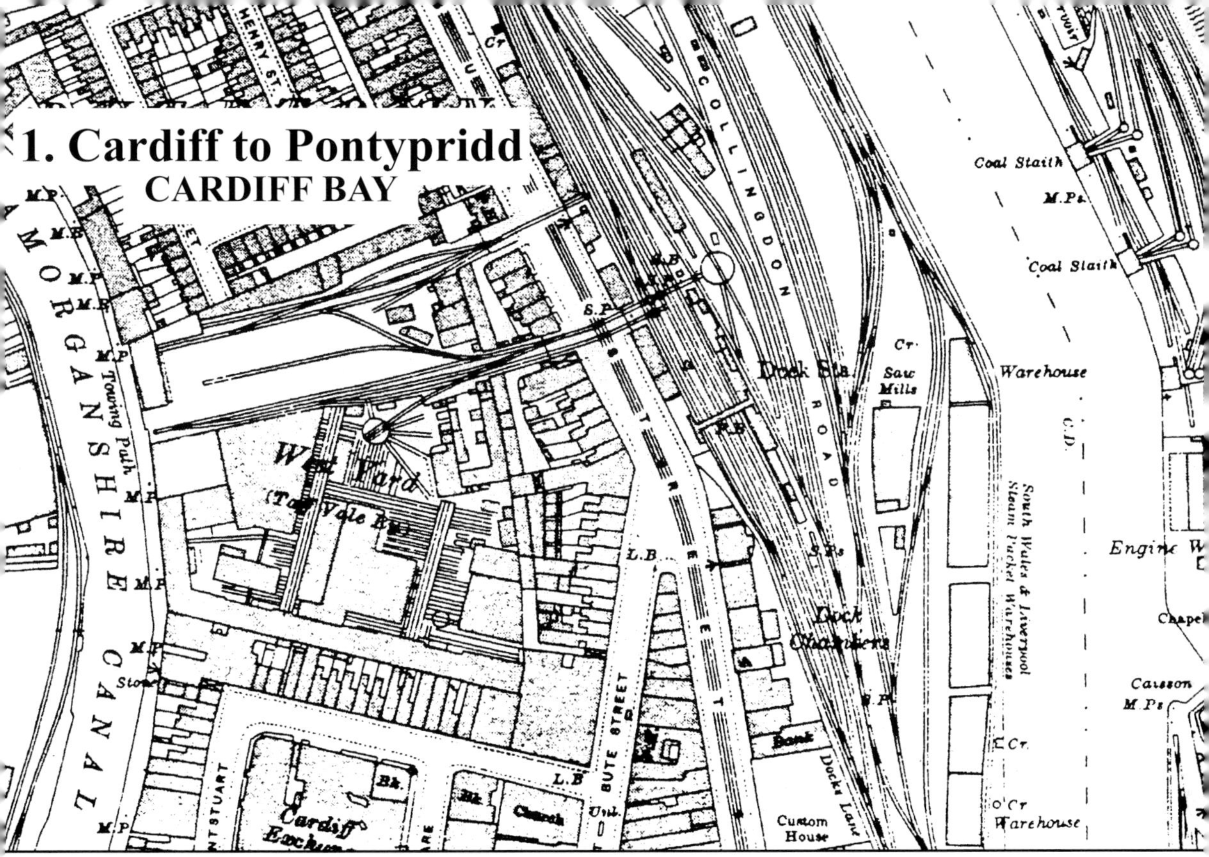

III. We start our journey inland where the TVR coal trains ended theirs. The contents were loaded into ships at Bute West Dock (left) and Bute East Dock, which is right of centre on this 1901 map at 12ins to 1 mile. The lines to the east of this dock were then GWR property and those in the top right corner were those of the Rhymney Railway, as was the engine shed shown. Dock Station of the TVR can be found on the left, near West Yard. The station was opened to passengers sometime between April 1841 and December 1844 and became Bute Road from 1st July 1924 until 21st September 1994, since when it has been Cardiff Bay. Bute West Dock (1839-1964) and Bute East Dock (1859-1970) have changed recently. The former has been infilled to allow building development and the latter remains as part of the water supply to Cardiff Docks.

IV. Trains from the former RR route began using Bute Road station in 1928. It is seen in more detail on this 1920 edition. The footbridge was added in 1879.

1. Two terminal platforms replaced the island one in 1929 and are seen in 1957. The building behind the locomotive was the headquarters of the TVR, built in 1843. (Stations UK)

2.   A view in the other direction in the same era has the signal box indistinct in the distance. It had 61 levers and was in use from 1927 until 1966. Only the platform on the left remained in use in 2002. It had been reduced to take only four coaches, but normally only received one. The ornate waiting room is noteworthy, but this was destroyed as was the canopy. (Stations UK)

Our *Cardiff to Dowlais* album contains other maps and pictures; the latter are numbered 4 to 6.

3.   The TVR offices have been listed Grade I and a replacement canopy created. Locomotive restoration was progressed under it and a railway museum was established indoors. However, all such activity was moved to Barry Island in 1994. This photograph was taken on 20th March 2011. (D.K.Jones)

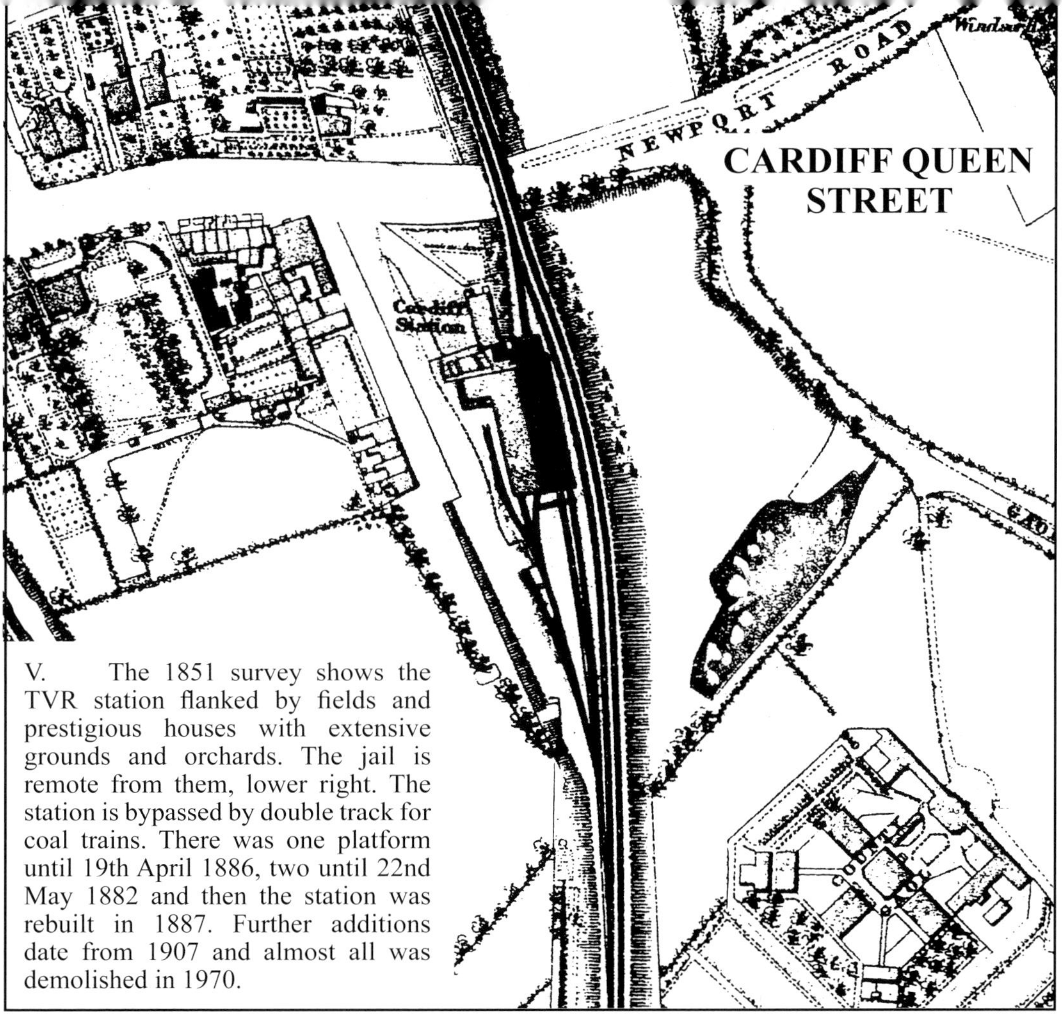

CARDIFF QUEEN STREET

V. The 1851 survey shows the TVR station flanked by fields and prestigious houses with extensive grounds and orchards. The jail is remote from them, lower right. The station is bypassed by double track for coal trains. There was one platform until 19th April 1886, two until 22nd May 1882 and then the station was rebuilt in 1887. Further additions date from 1907 and almost all was demolished in 1970.

4. An Edwardian postcard reveals the generous proportions of this busy station, which was well lit by gas and had wide staircases from street level. Lifts were added later. (Lens of Sutton coll.)

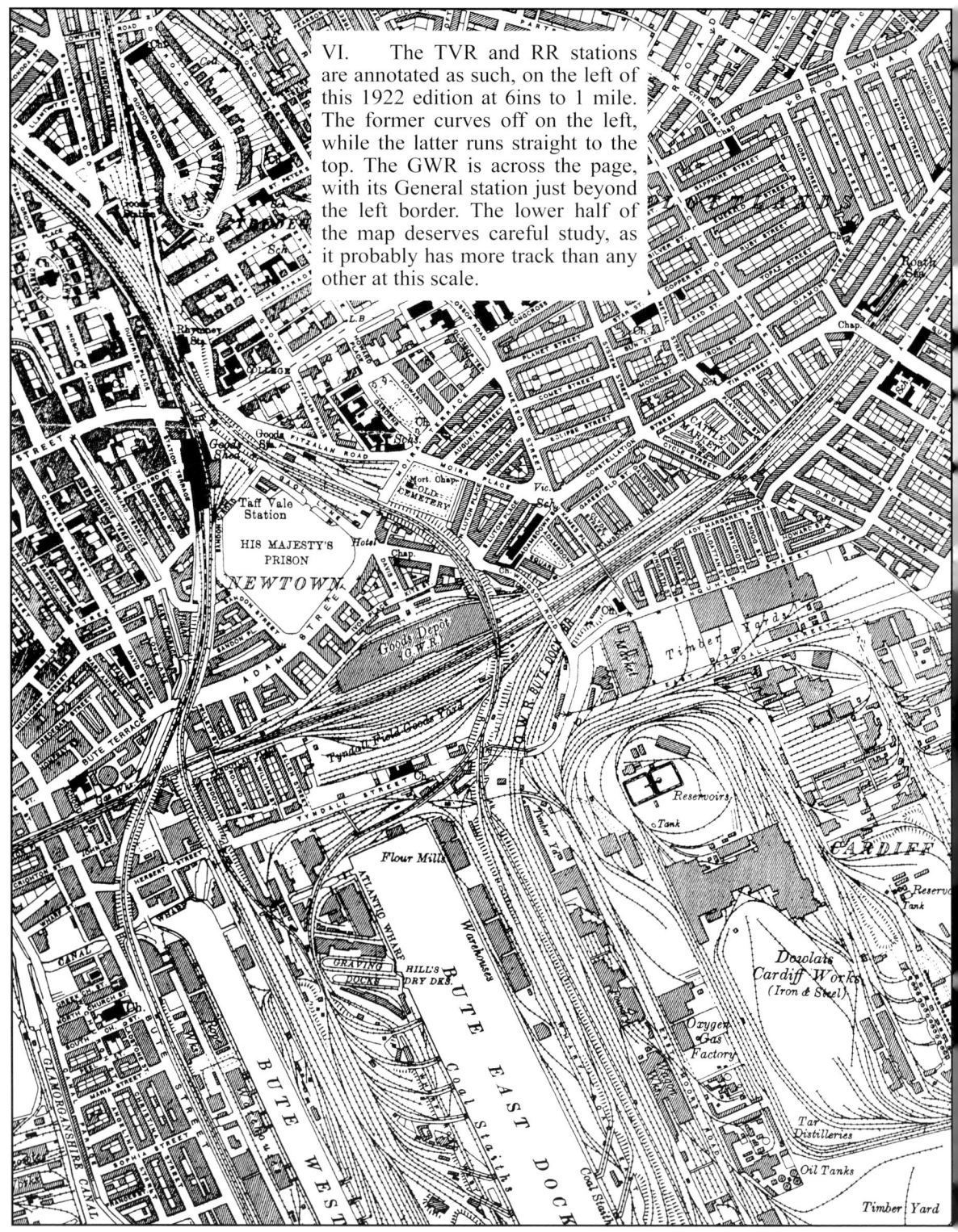

VI.   The TVR and RR stations are annotated as such, on the left of this 1922 edition at 6ins to 1 mile. The former curves off on the left, while the latter runs straight to the top. The GWR is across the page, with its General station just beyond the left border. The lower half of the map deserves careful study, as it probably has more track than any other at this scale.

➔   VII. The 1880 enlargement has Bute West Dock lower left, together with its connection to the Glamorganshire Canal on the left. Its link to Bute East Dock can also be found. An outpost of the London & North Western Railway can be seen in the form of a goods depot. Its traffic ran over the RR. The TVR continues north on the bottom of the next map. Its trains used the connection to the GWR regularly from June 1896.

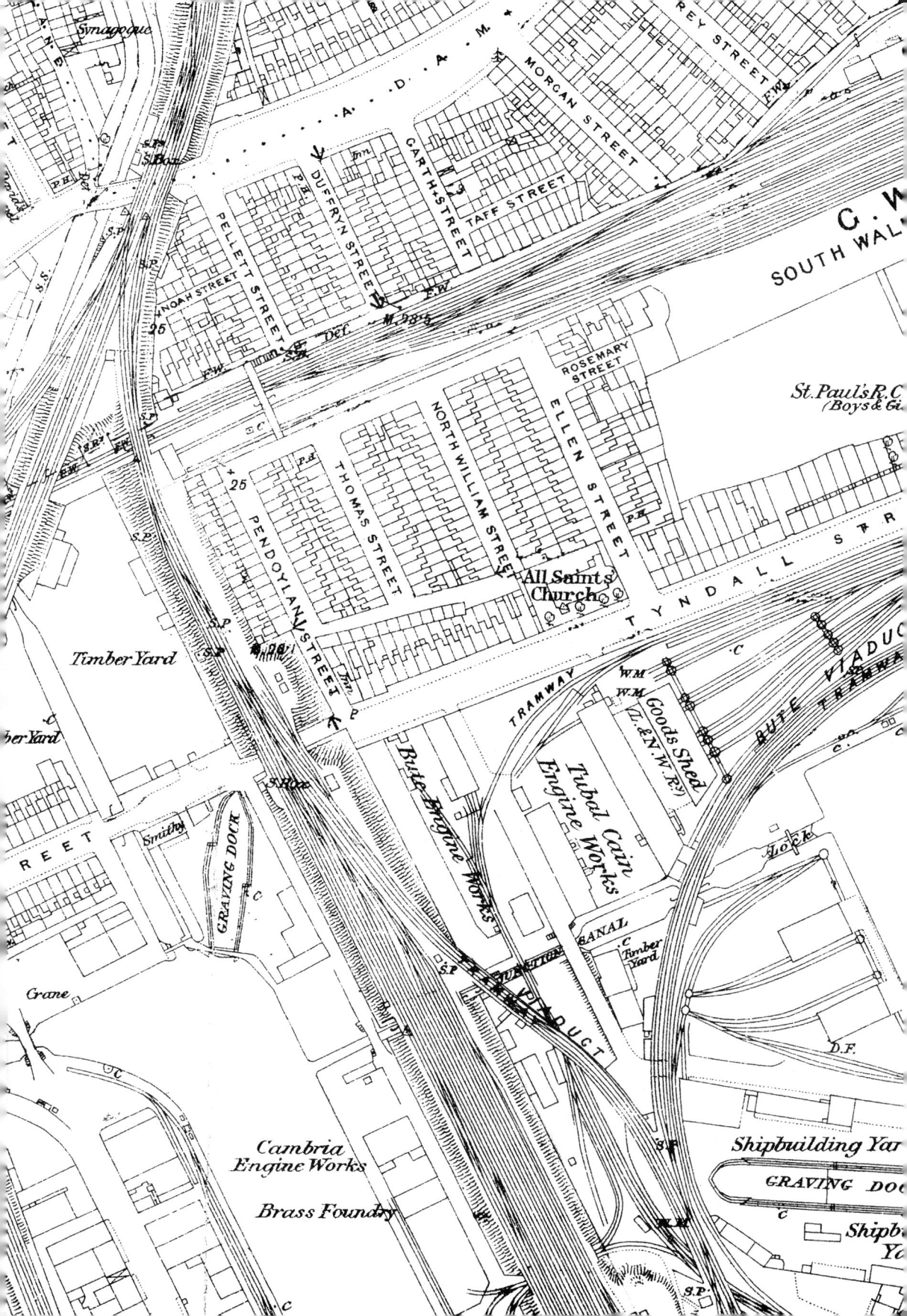

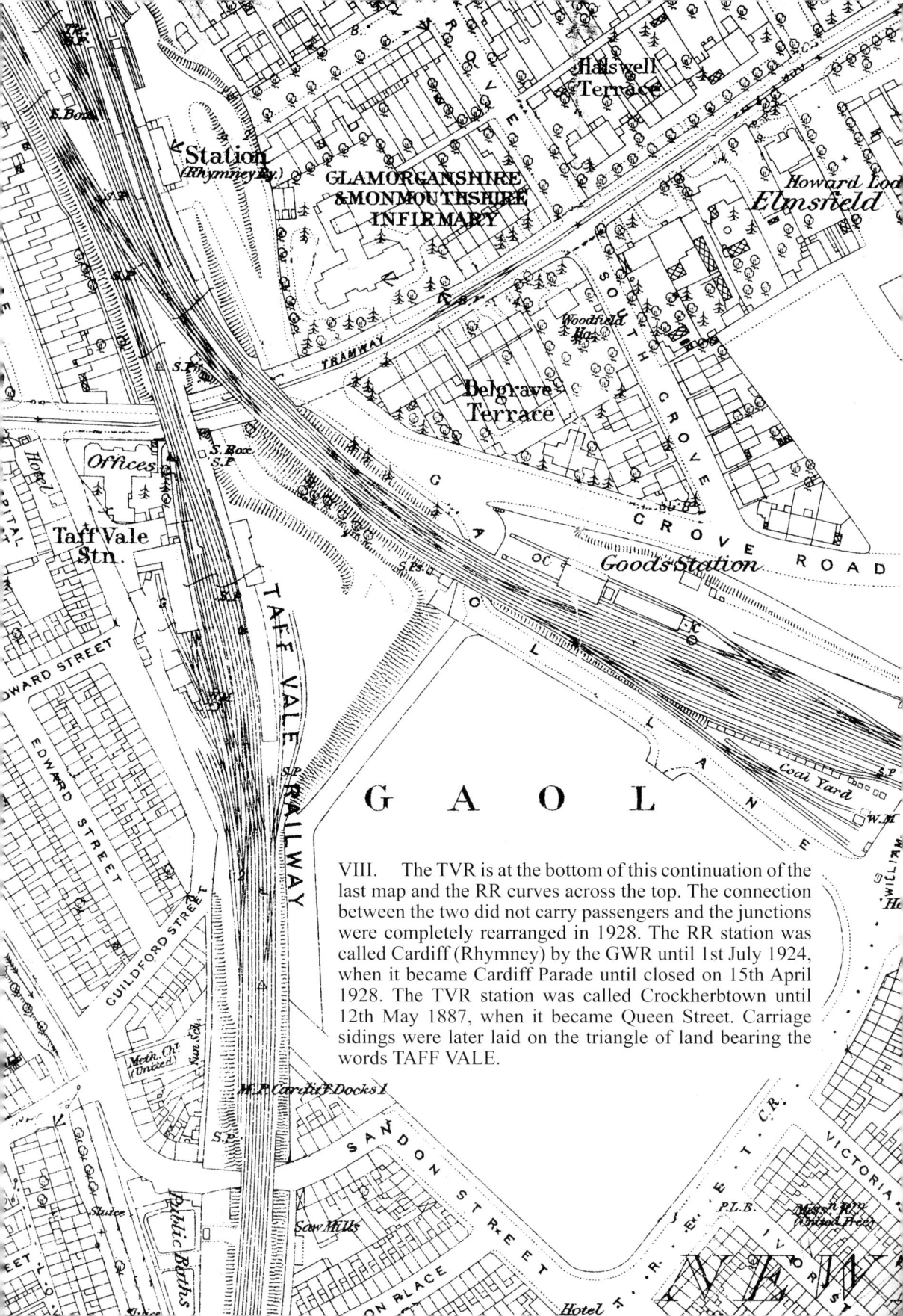

VIII.   The TVR is at the bottom of this continuation of the last map and the RR curves across the top. The connection between the two did not carry passengers and the junctions were completely rearranged in 1928. The RR station was called Cardiff (Rhymney) by the GWR until 1st July 1924, when it became Cardiff Parade until closed on 15th April 1928. The TVR station was called Crockherbtown until 12th May 1887, when it became Queen Street. Carriage sidings were later laid on the triangle of land bearing the words TAFF VALE.

5.   The smoke vents on the roof are seen more clearly from the south and also included is the canopy on the island platform. This came into use in the 1930s; the bay platform is on the left and was often used by trains to Bute Road. (Stations UK)

6.   We look south from the bay in May 1951 and in the adjacent siding are ex-TVR auto trailers. On the left is South Box, which had a 167-lever frame and was open from 1928 until 27th June 1966. (P.J.Garland/R.S.Carpenter)

7.   Further auto trailers are seen more fully on 5th May 1951 as 0-4-2T no. 1420 passes South Box. Engine cleaning was a low priority in those austere times. There was a shuttle service between Bute Street and Maindy North Road Halt from 1906 until 1958. (H.C.Casserley)

8.   The platforms are seen from the north on 17th August 1963, the island being on the far left. The end was nigh for the historic overall roof, rebuilding taking place in 1973-74. The official opening was on 17th July 1975. (P.J.Garland/R.S.Carpenter)

9. All the ancient structures were destroyed and this building was provided to house the ticket office and other facilities. It was recorded in May 2001, along with Brunel House (right), railway offices for many years. (B.W.L.Brooksbank)

10. Three of the five platform faces were retained, the left one being exclusively for Cardiff Bay trains. No. 121032 is working the 12-minute interval service on 13th February 2009. Similar single cars were still working the branch in 2011; three tracks then ran southwards. (V.Mitchell)

This area is featured in the Middleton Press album *Cardiff Trolleybuses* and the railways are in *Branch Lines around Barry, Cardiff to Dowlais, Cardiff to Swansea* and *Gloucester to Cardiff*.

NORTH OF CARDIFF QUEEN STREET

11.   North Box had 200 levers and is seen on 17th August 1963; it closed on 20th December 1964. The former TVR route to Llandaff is on the left and the ex-RR alignment is straight ahead. Cardiff Parade station had been on the right. (P.J.Garland/R.S.Carpenter)

12.   Simplification of the junction was completed on 1st May 1971 and a new, but narrower, bridge was put in place. A train for Penarth is passing over it on 14th August 2008. Queen Street itself begins under it. (H.Ballantyne)

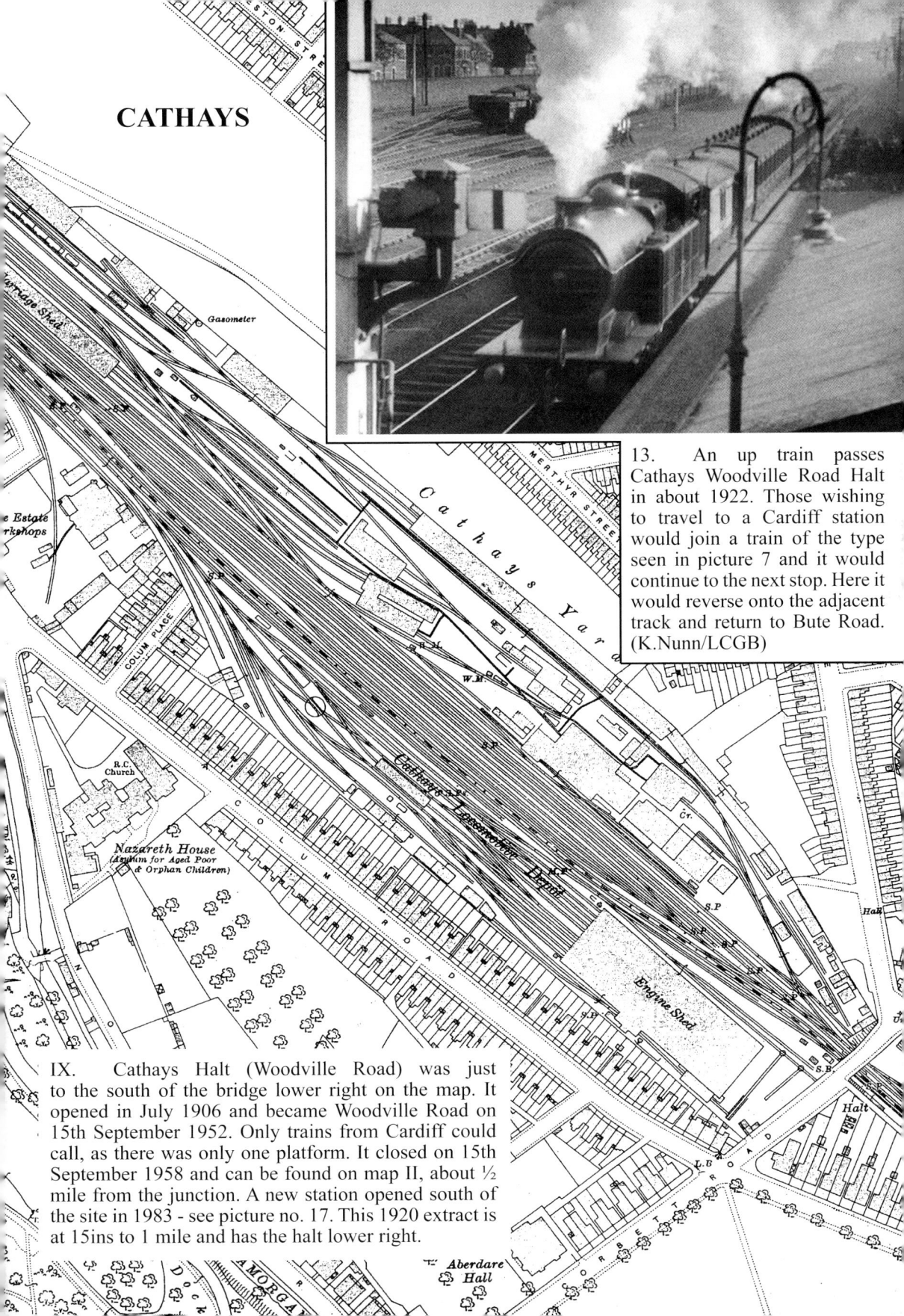

CATHAYS

13.   An up train passes Cathays Woodville Road Halt in about 1922. Those wishing to travel to a Cardiff station would join a train of the type seen in picture 7 and it would continue to the next stop. Here it would reverse onto the adjacent track and return to Bute Road. (K.Nunn/LCGB)

IX.   Cathays Halt (Woodville Road) was just to the south of the bridge lower right on the map. It opened in July 1906 and became Woodville Road on 15th September 1952. Only trains from Cardiff could call, as there was only one platform. It closed on 15th September 1958 and can be found on map II, about ½ mile from the junction. A new station opened south of the site in 1983 - see picture no. 17. This 1920 extract is at 15ins to 1 mile and has the halt lower right.

14.   The map shows the engine shed as rectangular, but the northern quarter is missing, it having been removed in 1938. The TVR brought a shed into use in 1884 and a coaling plant was added in 1929. There were 53 locomotives allocated here in 1947 and this smoky photograph was taken in about 1955. Steam hauled passenger services ceased here on 30th November 1957. (M.J.Stretton coll.)

15.   A new roof was provided in 1937-38, together with good smoke hoods. Seen on 6th May 1951 are ex-TVR 0-6-2T no. 390 and two ex-GWR engines, 0-4-2T no. 1420 and 0-6-0PT no. 3698. The shed was divided in 1959 to segregate the new diesels and closed in November 1964. (H.C.Casserley)

16.   A view towards Cardiff on 5th September 1957 includes 0-6-0PT no. 6408 and part of the ex-TVR carriage and wagon works. The track on the right leads to the engine shed. Its code was then 88A and it became 88M in March 1962. (D.K.Jones coll.)

17.   Cathays station was opened just south of the depots on 3rd October 1983 and is seen on 30th of that month as the 10.35 Treherbert to Barry DMU pulls in. The station improved access to the University of Cardiff and each platform was built to take four coaches and later extended for six coaches. (H.Ballantyne)

18.　　On the north side of the running lines was the wagon works, which undertook maintenance of track machines. It is seen on 16th February 1996, although it had closed on 18th March 1993. A shed had been opened in 1846 by the TVR in a corner of the site and was its carriage and wagon works. (M.J.Stretton)

MAINDY HALT

19.　　This halt, opened as Maindy North Road, was close to the A470 (see map II) and was in use from 1907 until 15th September 1958. The suffix North Road was dropped in 1952. 0-6-2T no. 5691 is working a five-coach stopping train on 25th May 1957. On the left is Maindy Bridge signal box, which opened in 1956 and closed on 27th June 1966. It had 54 levers. Further west was Maindy Fuel Signal Box from 1890 to 1966. The sidings served various firms until 1970, including a patent fuel firm. (S.Rickard/J&J coll.)

EAST OF LLANDAFF

20.   Roath Branch Junction Box is seen from a train from Cardiff on 26th June 1960. The branch was freight-only, mostly coal to Roath Docks, and is shown on map II. It closed on 6th May 1968, but the signal box had become a ground frame on 22nd July 1966. It survived as an office until the sidings closed in June 1981. (M.Dart/Transport Treasury)

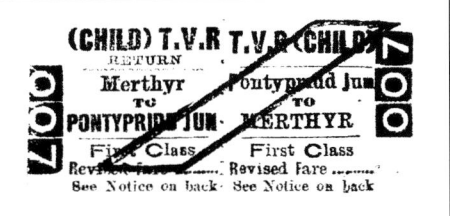

Llandaff	1923	1933
Passenger tickets issued	176827	82906
Season tickets issued	4475	7039
Parcels forwarded	17533	60320
General goods forwarded (tons)	187790	97
Coal and coke received (tons)	58346	3279
Other minerals received (tons)	41891	2406
General goods received (tons)	1583	233
Coal and coke handled	7483	2824
Trucks of livestock handled	33	2

LLANDAFF

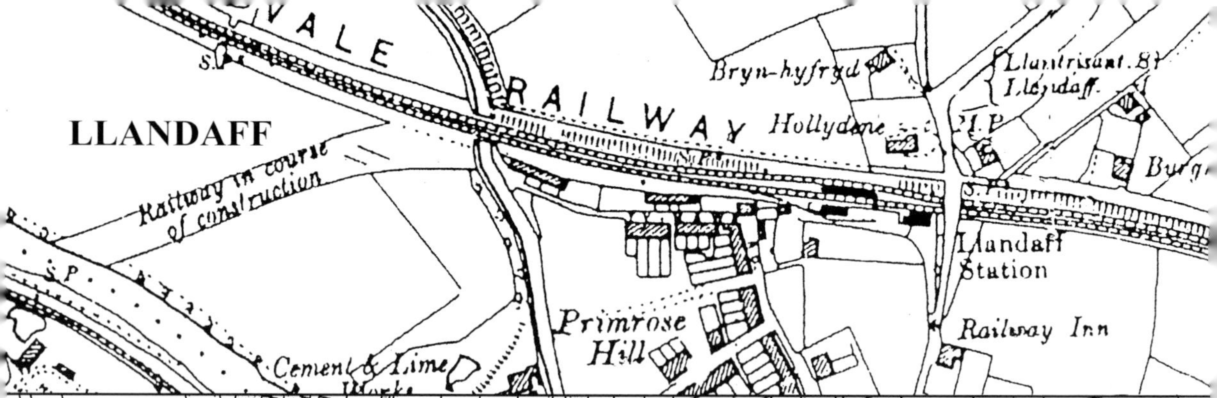

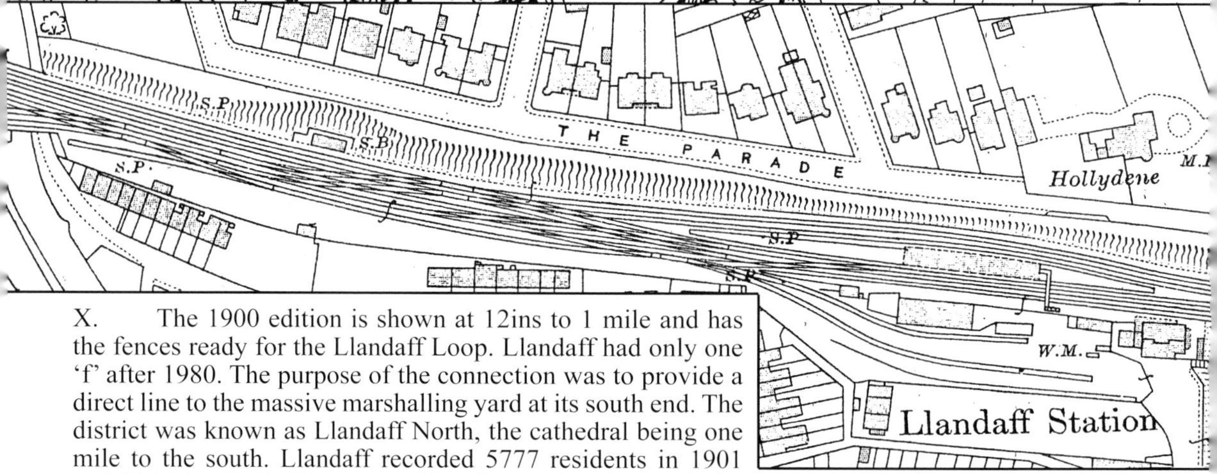

X. The 1900 edition is shown at 12ins to 1 mile and has the fences ready for the Llandaff Loop. Llandaff had only one 'f' after 1980. The purpose of the connection was to provide a direct line to the massive marshalling yard at its south end. The district was known as Llandaff North, the cathedral being one mile to the south. Llandaff recorded 5777 residents in 1901 and 22,164 in 1961. There were 16 or 17 employees here in the 1930s. The lower map is from 1920.

21. The 17.50 Merthyr to Barry Island DMU arrives on 25th May 1973. The goods lines are just visible through the fence netting. They were subject to "permissive working", which meant that the driver had to look out for the train ahead. They were singled in July 1973 and the remaining one closed in June 1981. (T.Heavyside)

LLANDAF

22.   A view towards Cardiff on 8th April 1984 shows some of the former station building high up on the left. The suffix "for Whitchurch" was used from 20th October 1896 until 12th May 1980. The steel road bridge was provided in 1903 to span four tracks. (D.K.Jones coll.)

23.   Looking the other way on the same day, we see that Llandaff Loop is still signalled. However, the goods yard had closed on 27th June 1966, having been used for coal traffic only for seven months. It had a 3-ton crane and there had been two private sidings. The signal box was called Llandaff Loop and functioned from 1900 until 12th May 1998. Its 80 lever frame was reduced to 40 in May 1966. (D.K.Jones coll.)

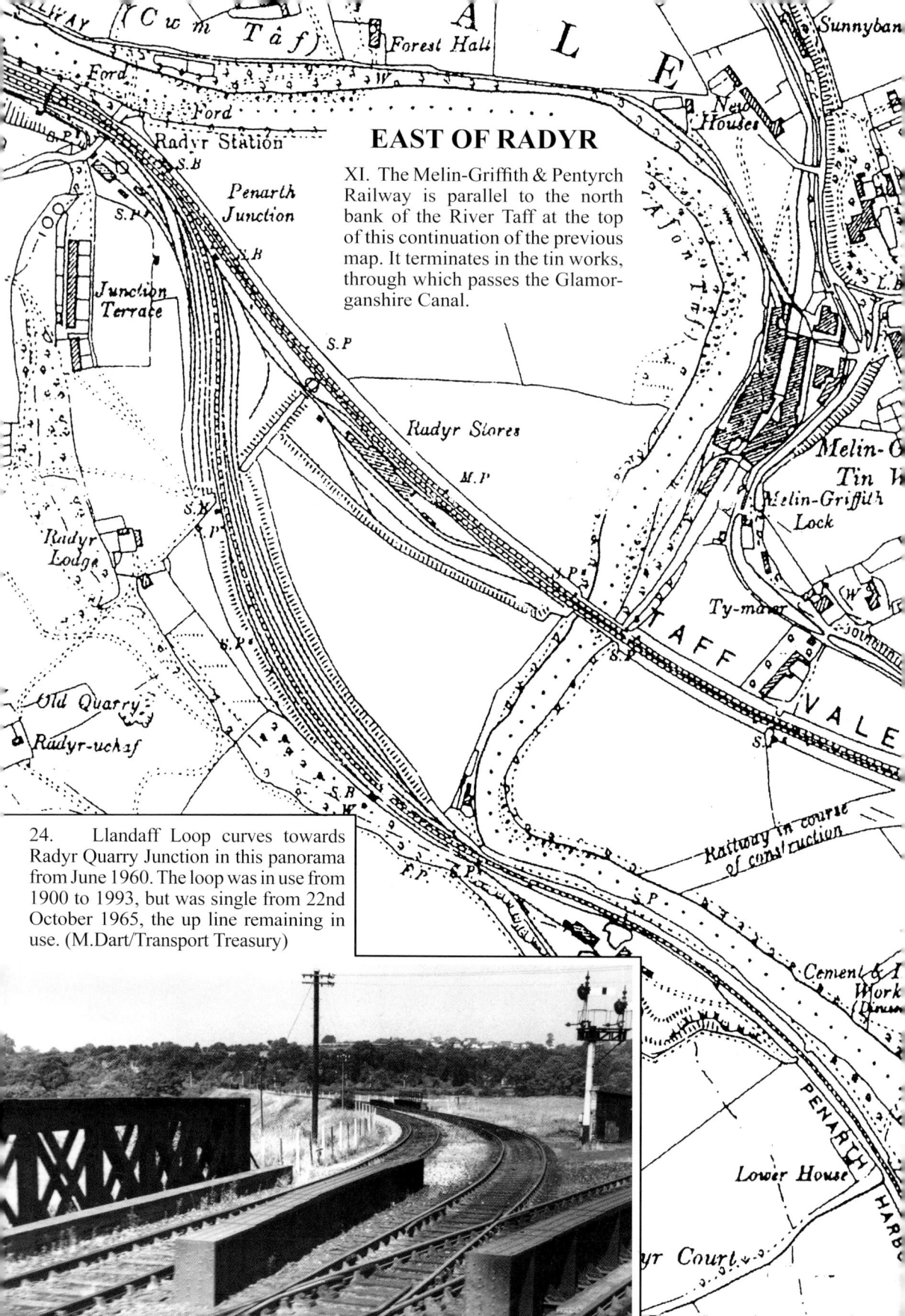

EAST OF RADYR

XI. The Melin-Griffith & Pentyrch Railway is parallel to the north bank of the River Taff at the top of this continuation of the previous map. It terminates in the tin works, through which passes the Glamorganshire Canal.

24. Llandaff Loop curves towards Radyr Quarry Junction in this panorama from June 1960. The loop was in use from 1900 to 1993, but was single from 22nd October 1965, the up line remaining in use. (M.Dart/Transport Treasury)

RADYR

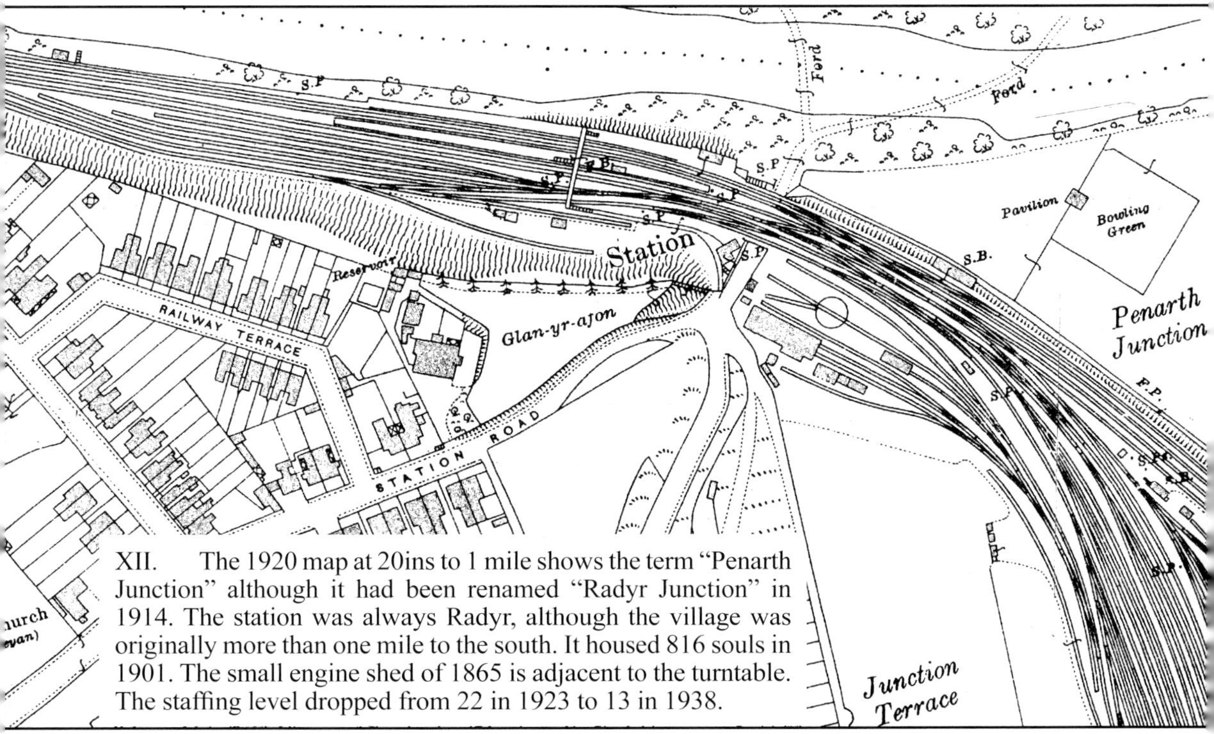

XII. The 1920 map at 20ins to 1 mile shows the term "Penarth Junction" although it had been renamed "Radyr Junction" in 1914. The station was always Radyr, although the village was originally more than one mile to the south. It housed 816 souls in 1901. The small engine shed of 1865 is adjacent to the turntable. The staffing level dropped from 22 in 1923 to 13 in 1938.

25. The station opened long after the line, on 1st June 1883 and was featured on an Edwardian postcard. The lines to Llandaff are in the right foreground and the Penarth tracks diverge from them. The station buildings are on the left and all passengers had to use the footbridge or the subway, known here as the underpass. (Lens of Sutton coll.)

Radyr	1923	1933
Passenger tickets issued	65043	45368
Season tickets issued	792	1141
Parcels forwarded	3188	3018
General goods forwarded (tons)	1366	860
Coal and coke received (tons)	71598	937
Other minerals received (tons)	3344	951
General goods received (tons)	2434	381
Coal and coke handled	546	751
Trucks of livestock handled	-	-

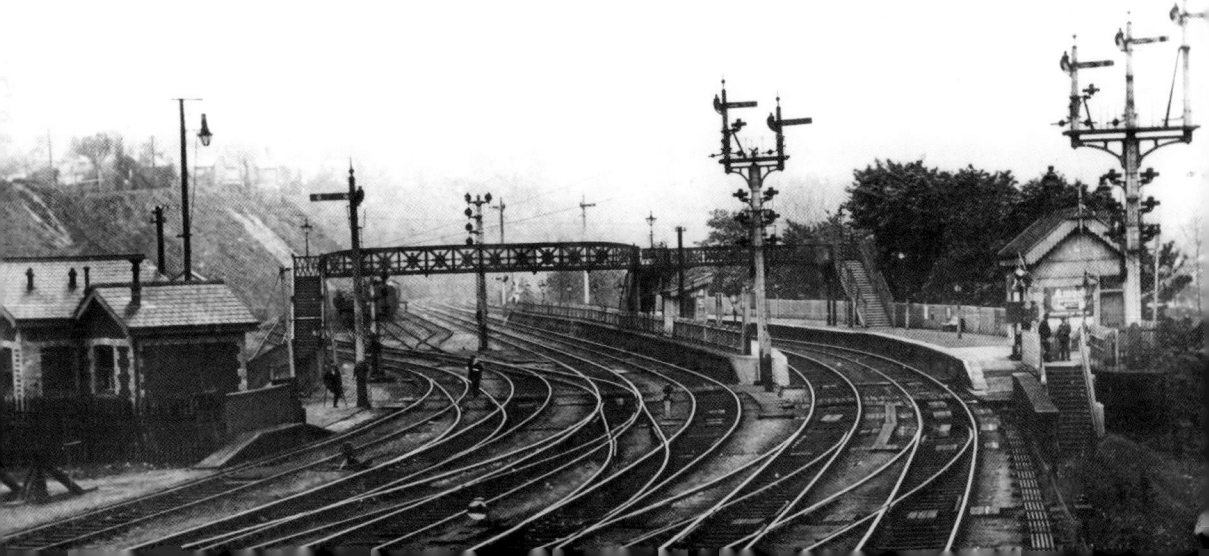

26.   This is the panorama covering the lower right corner of the map, as seen from the signal box (S.B.) in May 1943. The marshalling yard was begun in 1860, grew steadily and closed in 1994 to eventually become a housing estate. A class 4300 2-6-0 waits on the right, while an 0-6-2T blows off on the left. The water tank is above the coal stage and only a fragment of the adjacent engine shed can be seen. (GWR)

27.   The four-road engine shed was completed in 1931 and in 1947 was housing 28 locomotives, mostly 0-6-2Ts. These worked coal trains from the valleys and larger engines took over on trips to English cities. The ash plant is nearest us in this 1943 view and the nearby chimney is on the sand drier. The shed closed in March 1965 and was leased to Powell Dyffryn Wagon Co. Ltd from October 1968. They used it for wagon repairs until the 1990s. (GWR)

28.	The entrance to the goods yard is on the right of this eastward view from 5th May 1951. No. 41 is an ex-RR 0-6-2T, which was built by Beyer Peacock in 1921. The up platform would take five coaches and the down one six. (R.M.Casserley)

29.	The two tracks to the right of the fence are the relief lines and stabling sidings are beyond. These later became loops. The signal box lasted from 1897 until 1961. (R.M.Casserley)

30.   The new signal box opened on 4th June 1961. It was originally erected at Swindon Station East, but not commissioned. Its 107-lever frame had a busy time with coal traffic, as witnessed from the footbridge on 25th March 1973. No. 6918 waits to enter the marshalling yard, as no. 3420 approaches on the right. (T.Heavyside)

31.   The goods yard had been on the extreme left, but it closed on 6th January 1964. The remaining sidings had become loops, but were lifted in 1983 to make way for a car park. No. 6918 is on the down relief line on 4th June 1961. (T.Heavyside)

32.	It is 16th February 1996 and on the left no. 150278 is working the 13.52 Merthyr to Penarth whilst on the right is the 14.07 Penarth to Treherbert, formed of no. 150275. Such trains ran via Cardiff; there had never been a regular direct service. The signals would last only months, the box closing on 12th May 1998. (M.J.Stretton)

33.	The fence on the up platform was removed, so that an additional face could be provided and the track layout revised for increased line speeds. It came into use on 24th May 1998 and is seen on 13th February 2009, with the 10.04 Radyr to Cardiff Central. No. 150283 is arriving, forming the 09.17 Treherbert to Barry Island. The car park had come to be useful. (V.Mitchell)

PENTYRCH

34. The station was open from 9th October 1840 until 22nd June 1863 and appears on the earliest timetable in this album. It was replaced later by new stations at Radyr and Walnut Tree Junction. (A.Dudman coll.)

XIII. The crossing and connection are shown on the 1920 edition.

35. Two DMUs destined for Barry Island pass the station house on 10th July 1959. The leading unit is on the crossing seen in the next pictures. (S.Rickard/J&J coll.)

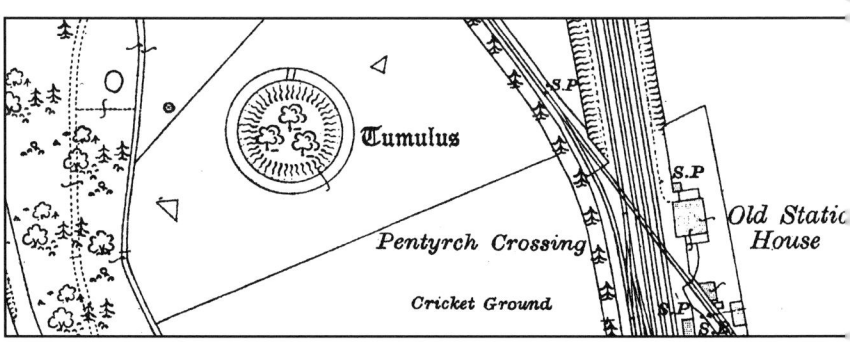

Tumulus

Pentyrch Crossing

Cricket Ground

Old Station House

36.   Melin-Griffith Tin Works and its railway have been seen on map XI and here it crosses the main line on the level. The signal box was called Pentyrch Crossing and is also seen in the previous picture. It was open from 1901 until 7th October 1962 and latterly had 39 levers.
(M.Dart/Transport Treasury)

37.   This and the previous photograph were taken in June 1960 and here we see part of the firm's private siding for traffic exchange, left. There was another connection to it behind the camera. It originally ran to Pentyrch Upper Iron Works, but by the early 1940s only served Ty-nant Quarry Siding. The lines were removed in 1961. (M.Dart/Transport Treasury)

SOUTH OF TAFFS WELL

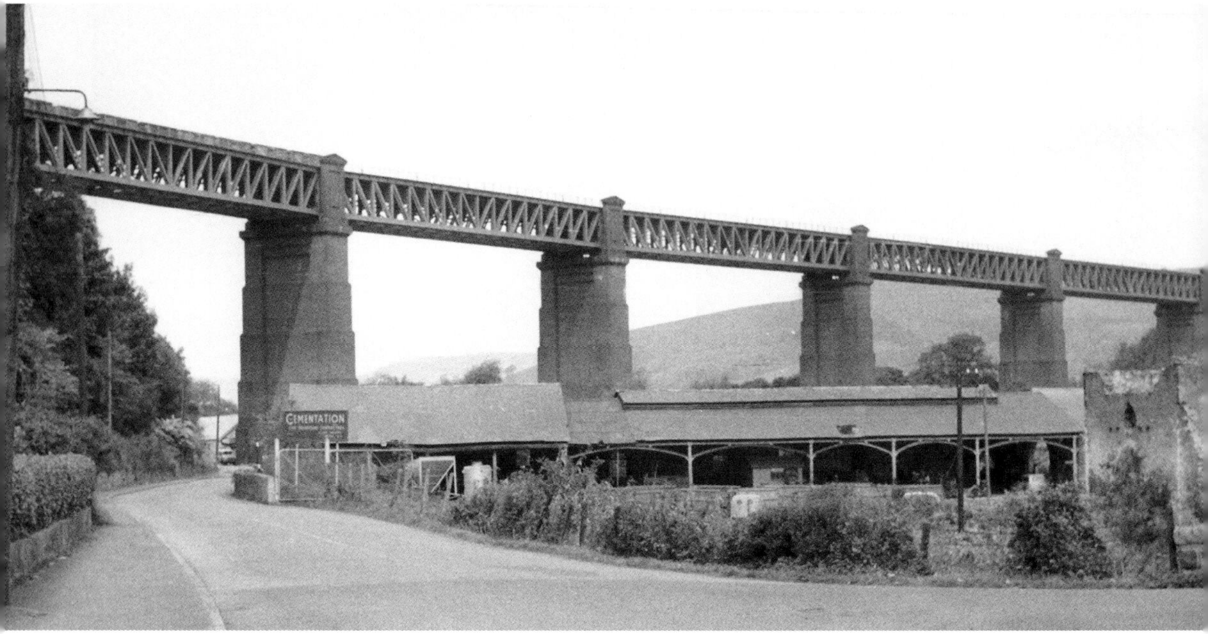

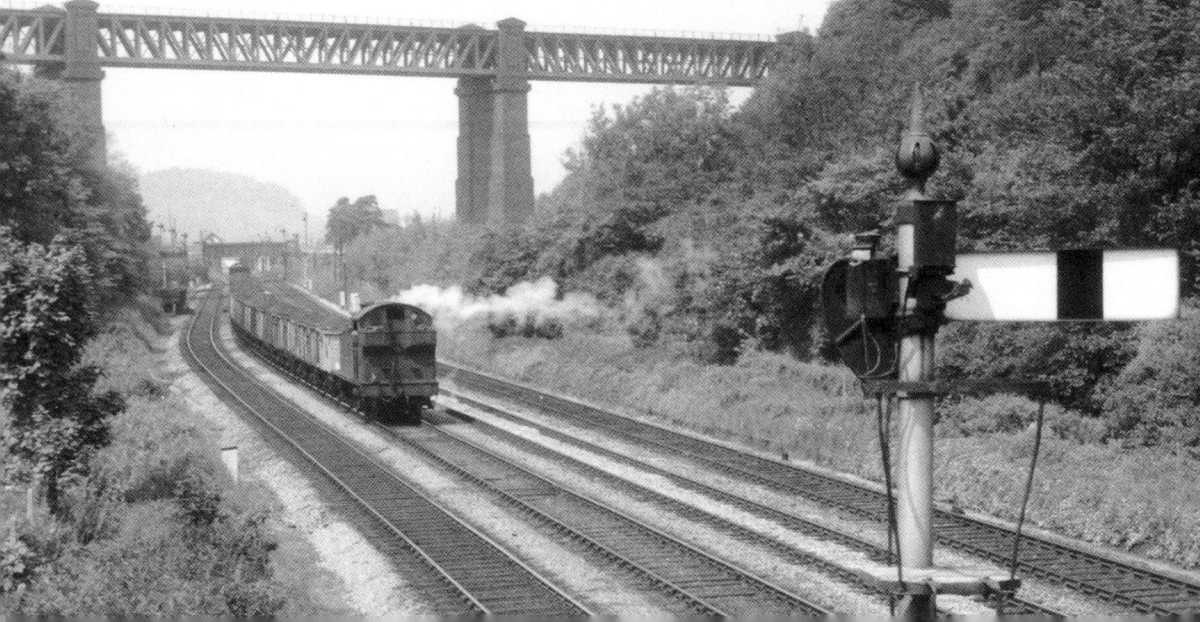

38. Seen on 2nd September 1959 is the Walnut Tree Viaduct (516yds) which had seven steel lattice girder spans up to 120ft high and carried the erstwhile Barry Railway's Caerphilly Branch across the Taff Vale. The viaduct closed to passenger traffic from July 1963 and was kept in use for local quarry traffic until December 1967. This was principally dolomite for use in the steelworks. Some freight wagons stand on the span above the road. The buildings in the foreground were formally the Pentyrch Iron Works. (S.P.Derek)

39. An 0-6-2T takes coal to the docks sometime in 1963. It is running on the down relief line and the A470 road bridge is in the background. The steelwork of the viaduct was dismantled in 1969. (D.K.Jones coll.)

40.　　A class 37 runs north with empties in bad weather on 24th August 1983, alongside the new highways which had necessitated the demolition of most of the viaduct piers in 1973. The relief lines northern limit is evident. (P.G.Barnes)

41.　　It is 31st March 1988 and no. 37162 is taking coal to Radyr marshalling yard. Castell Coch overlooks the entire gap in the hills in this area and has a thermal spring nearby. The name means red castle and it was created on a 12th century fort site in Gothic style in 1875-85 by the then Lord Bute, using a local red sandstone. (H.Ballantyne)

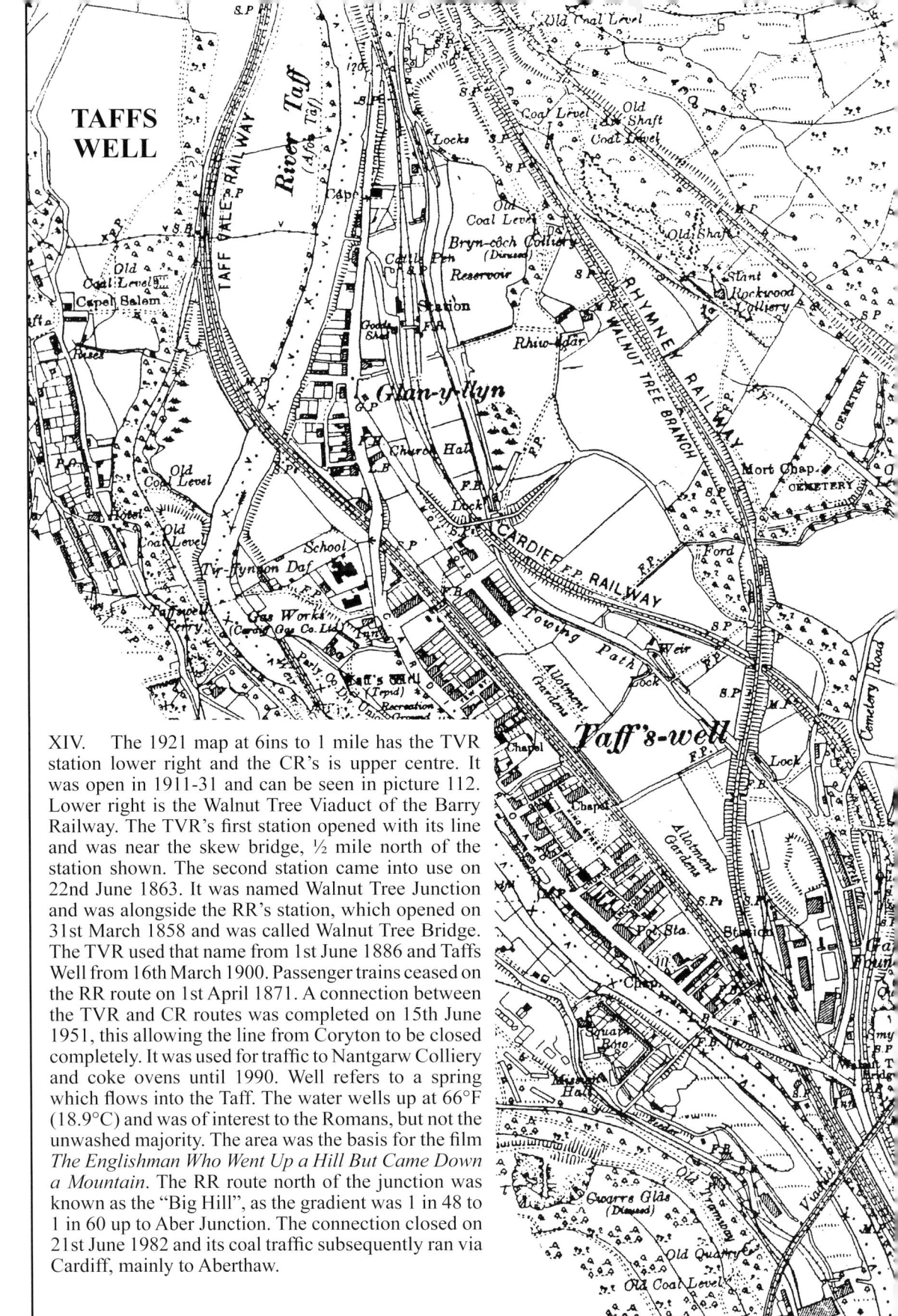

TAFFS WELL

XIV.   The 1921 map at 6ins to 1 mile has the TVR station lower right and the CR's is upper centre. It was open in 1911-31 and can be seen in picture 112. Lower right is the Walnut Tree Viaduct of the Barry Railway. The TVR's first station opened with its line and was near the skew bridge, ½ mile north of the station shown. The second station came into use on 22nd June 1863. It was named Walnut Tree Junction and was alongside the RR's station, which opened on 31st March 1858 and was called Walnut Tree Bridge. The TVR used that name from 1st June 1886 and Taffs Well from 16th March 1900. Passenger trains ceased on the RR route on 1st April 1871. A connection between the TVR and CR routes was completed on 15th June 1951, this allowing the line from Coryton to be closed completely. It was used for traffic to Nantgarw Colliery and coke ovens until 1990. Well refers to a spring which flows into the Taff. The water wells up at 66°F (18.9°C) and was of interest to the Romans, but not the unwashed majority. The area was the basis for the film *The Englishman Who Went Up a Hill But Came Down a Mountain*. The RR route north of the junction was known as the "Big Hill", as the gradient was 1 in 48 to 1 in 60 up to Aber Junction. The connection closed on 21st June 1982 and its coal traffic subsequently ran via Cardiff, mainly to Aberthaw.

42.   We look north up Taff Vale and see the TVR running straight into the distance from the station. The RR Walnut Tree Branch curves away on the right and a goods yard is lower right. The building is the RR engine shed, which closed in September 1922 and became part of Garth Works. The sign displayed by "The Junction" public house outside the station had the coat of arms of the Rhymney Railway on one side and that of the Taff Vale Railway on the other, symbolising the physical junction effected nearby. (Lens of Sutton coll.)

43.   The viaduct is in the background as 0-6-2T no. 6612 takes the up relief line behind the signal box on 27th August 1953. On the right is the smaller part of the goods yard; freight ceased on 27th June 1966. (S.Rickard/J&J coll.)

44.   Running through the down platform, on 10th June 1955 is a coal train hauled by 0-6-2T no. 5627. The curved track provided the link with Caerphilly and Aber Junction. There was an average of 27 men here in the 1930s. (S.Rickard/J&J coll.)

45.   A view south from the footbridge on 13th July 1958 includes the larger part of the goods yard on the left. The signal box was called Walnut Tree Junction and was in use until 25th January 1997. It had 79 levers and the top section was moved to Lydney on the Dean Forest Railway. (H.C.Casserley)

Taffs Well	1923	1933
Passenger tickets issued	110792	34301
Season tickets issued	2663	1765
Parcels forwarded	7631	8264
General goods forwarded (tons)	23576	18934
Coal and coke received (tons)	-	19052
Other minerals received (tons)	38231	18877
General goods received (tons)	10121	4510
Coal and coke handled	82738	6900
Trucks of livestock handled	2	-

46. Seen from an up DMU in about 1961 is 0-6-2T no. 5607 on the up relief line. At that time, the local population was 3083. The line over the viaduct was in use from 1901 to 1967. (S.Rickard/J&J coll.)

47. This splendid panorama is from the viaduct on 14th May 1965 and it features no. D6935 with a coal train from Aber Junction. The 1952 connection for Nantgarw traffic has two curves, top left. (H.Ballantyne)

48. The first signal box here had opened by 1867 and was in the lower left corner of this photograph, being high enough for the signalman to see over the road bridge. The down relief line was in use until 1968 and the up one to 1978. This view is from the road bridge on 16th May 1968 and includes DMUs passing. This took place at 24 and 54 minutes past most hours. (J.C.Gillham)

49. Looking south from the footbridge on 4th October 1969, we find that the A470 bridge had been upgraded, but that the viaduct was in terminal decline. The trackbed of the CR is at our level, on the left half of the picture. (J.C.Gillham)

50.   It is 24th September 1980 and no. 37271 trundles south with empties as nature takes over the relief lines and elsewhere. Both platforms could take seven coaches. (D.H.Mitchell)

51.   The 14.52 from Merthyr Tydfil to Penarth was recorded on 16th February 1996. New roads and buildings had totally altered the landscape, but the Sprinters had improved train performance. (M.J.Stretton)

NORTH OF TAFFS WELL

52.   When the connection to the ex-CR line was added in 1952, suitably antique signals were used so that drivers could see them under the footbridge. The track curves to the right and is seen from the north end of the up platform on 16th February 1996. The branch had closed on 26th February 1988. In the distance is the skew bridge, which had been rebuilt in 1992. (M.J.Stretton)

TREFOREST ESTATE

53.   The halt was opened for factory workers on 5th January 1942 and appeared in public timetables from May 1946. We look north in the 1960s, with the freight lines on the left. Access was by two subways under the down line.
(Lens of Sutton coll.)

54. The relief lines had gone by the time a photographer had arrived in 1976. The stop continues to serve a large industrial estate and is shown between the words TAFF VALE on map II. A nine coach train could be accommodated each side. (D.K.Jones coll.)

55. Map II also gives an indication of the length of the sidings serving the estate. One reached Upper Boat Power Station. Maesmawr Signal Box controlled access to the network and is seen in 1983. It opened in 1930 and its 65-lever frame was taken out of use on 27th January 1997. The box was moved to the Dean Forest Railway. (P.Jones)

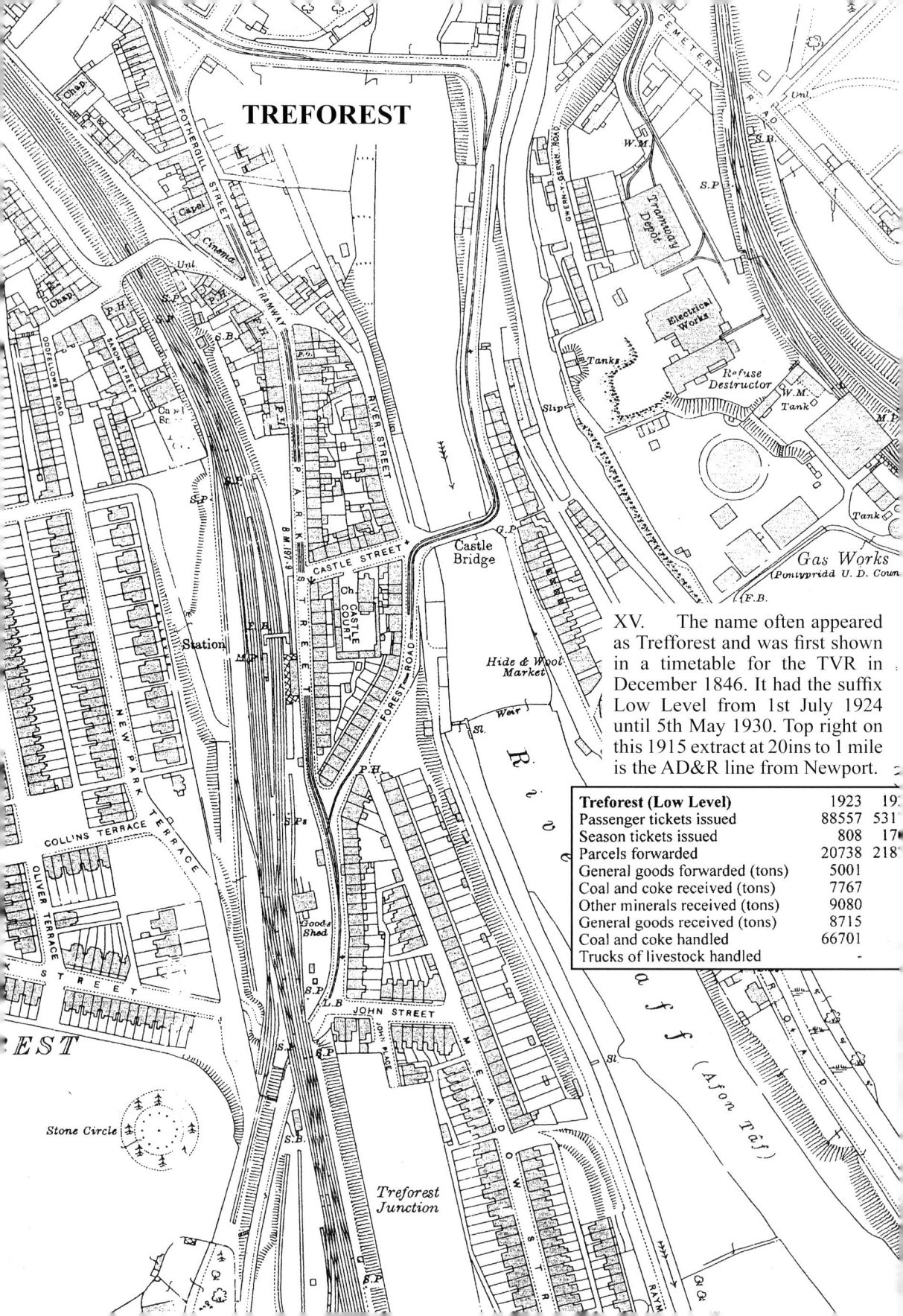

TREFOREST

XV.   The name often appeared as Trefforest and was first shown in a timetable for the TVR in December 1846. It had the suffix Low Level from 1st July 1924 until 5th May 1930. Top right on this 1915 extract at 20ins to 1 mile is the AD&R line from Newport.

Treforest (Low Level)	1923	19
Passenger tickets issued	88557	531
Season tickets issued	808	17
Parcels forwarded	20738	218
General goods forwarded (tons)	5001	
Coal and coke received (tons)	7767	
Other minerals received (tons)	9080	
General goods received (tons)	8715	
Coal and coke handled	66701	
Trucks of livestock handled	-	

56.   This northward view is from June 1922. The up side waiting room was replaced by a brick built hut in the 1970s. The platforms could take seven coaches each. (D.K.Jones coll.)

57.   This autotrain will have just called at Church Village Halt and is using the crossovers opposite Treforest Junction signal box after the steep descent down from Tonteg on 2nd May 1959. The box is shown near the bottom of the map. It ceased to function on 10th June 1970 and had 84 levers. (D.K.Jones coll.)

58. No. 6438 is working the 5.31pm Cardiff Clarence Road to Pontypridd via St. Fagans on 3rd September 1960. It was a circuitous route for residents here. Staff numbers were 32 in 1923 and down to 18 in 1935. (D.K.Jones coll.)

59. A southward panorama in June 1960 has the relief lines in the centre and the goods yard on the right. The station has served the University of Glamorgan in more recent years. (M.Dart)

60.   A closer view in the same direction in the mid-1960s includes the up side brick shelter. Sadly the down side was lost later to a simple brick structure. (Lens of Sutton coll.)

61.   More car parking became possible after track clearance. No. 37301 runs through with ballast and coal from Aberdare, bound for Radyr marshalling yard, sometime in 1981. (P.Jones)

PONTYPRIDD

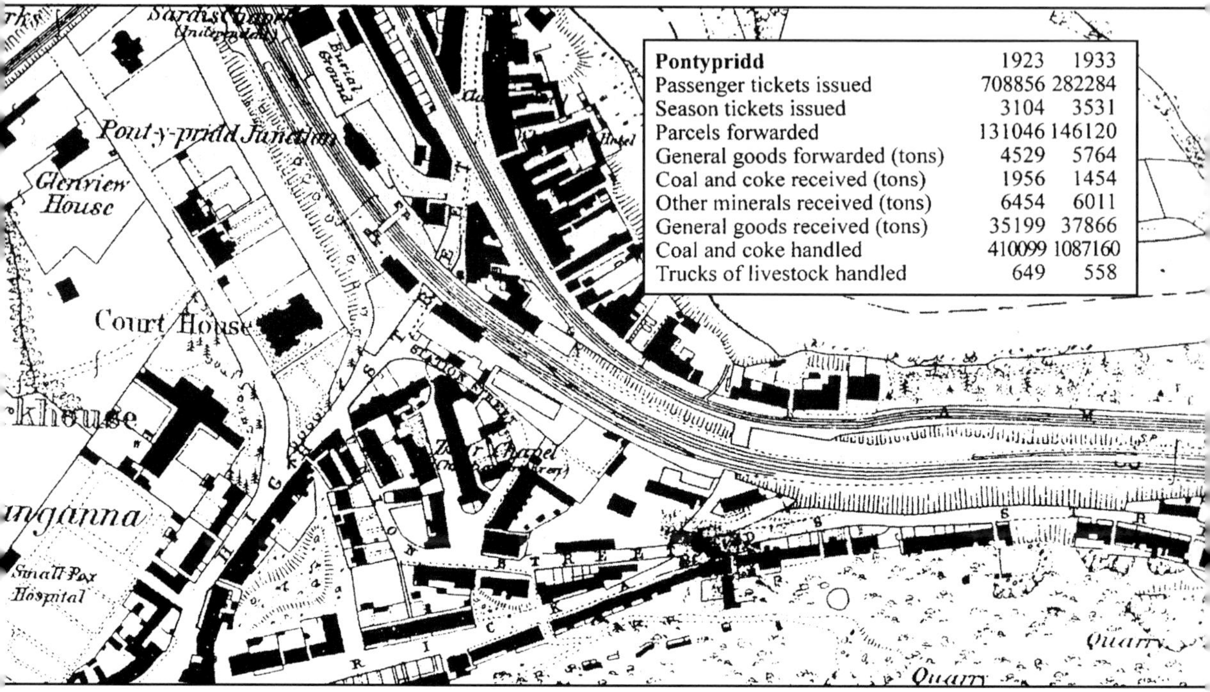

Pontypridd	1923	1933
Passenger tickets issued	708856	282284
Season tickets issued	3104	3531
Parcels forwarded	131046	146120
General goods forwarded (tons)	4529	5764
Coal and coke received (tons)	1956	1454
Other minerals received (tons)	6454	6011
General goods received (tons)	35199	37866
Coal and coke handled	410099	1087160
Trucks of livestock handled	649	558

XVI.   The 1874 edition has the horse-worked Thomas Tramway between the TVR and the River Taff. The station buildings are adjacent to the High Street and a single siding is to the right of it. The station was named Newbridge initially, Newbridge Junction from about 1862 until 1902, when it became Pontypridd. In 1924 it became Pontypridd Central and finally Pontypridd again in 1930. The tramway was worked by horses until 1905, when Pontypridd UDC electrified the 3ft 6ins gauge system and ran it until 1931.

62.   Brunel's chalet style buildings are seen in this southward view, prior to the rebuilding of 1891. Shunting horses were used into the 1950s. (GWR)

63. The rebuilding resulted in two long through platforms taking 12 coaches each, with short bays each end. At the north end on 11th September 1951 is 0-6-0PT no. 6411, ready to depart for Ynysybwl from platform 4. (R.M.Casserley)

64. We are looking south on 21st May 1955 as a 2-6-2T propels an autocoach on its journey to Caerphilly. It will soon diverge left at the junction shown on map XXXI, near picture 108. To the left of the camera was P.C&N Junction Box, which had 81 levers and was in use until 13th June 1970. (F.Hornby coll.)

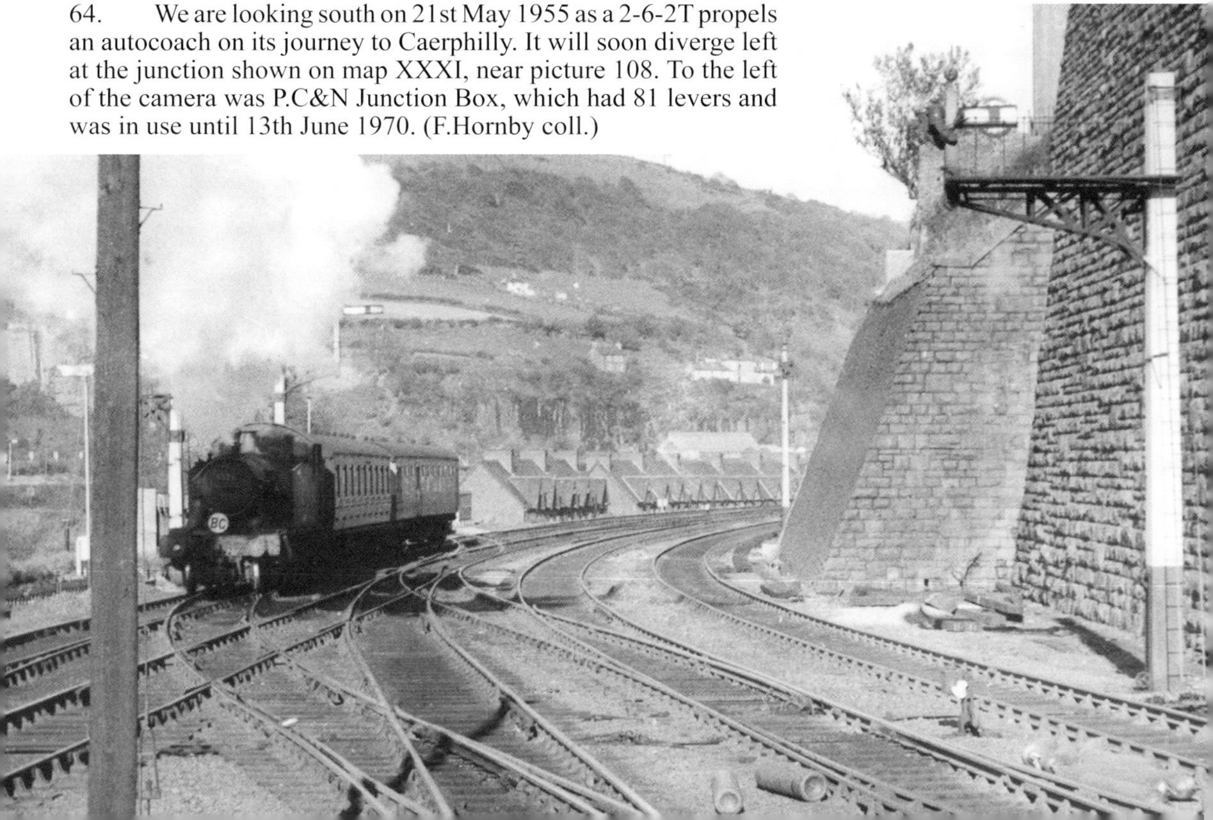

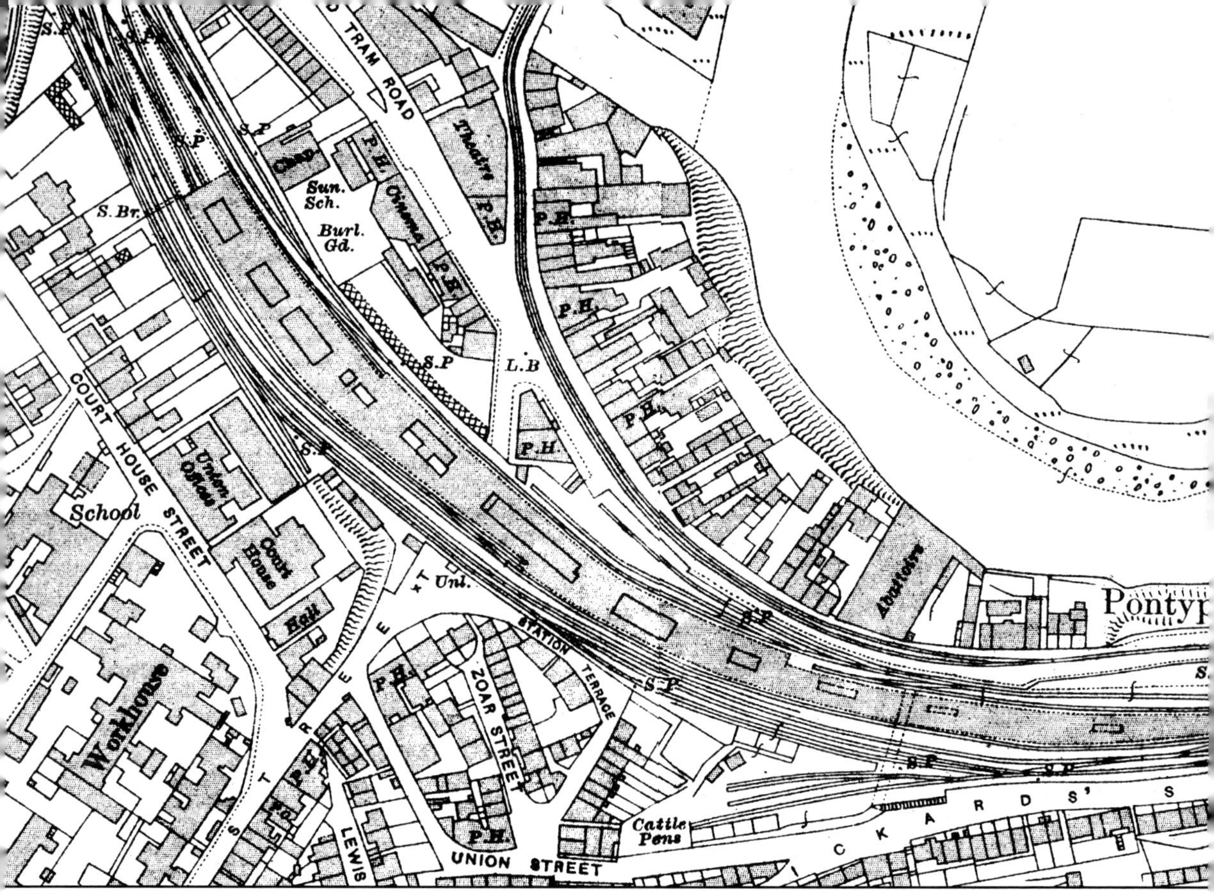

XVII. The 1919 survey details the massive changes which took place during the rebuilding of 1906-07. The junction of the Merthyr and Rhondda lines was north of the river until 1860, when a second viaduct was built and the junction was moved south of the Taff.

65.   Arriving on 2nd May 1959 is an 0-6-0PT with an autocoach from Cardiff Clarence Road, which has run via St. Fagans and Creigiau. Platform 1 is on the left and 6 on the right, in the distance. (S.C.L.Philips/D.K.Jones coll.)

66.   Resting at the north end of the station on 9th September 1960 is 0-6-0PT no. 6438 and we can examine some of the junction signals. The object on the left was called a fire devil and it prevented the water column from freezing. (S.Rickard/J&J coll.)

67.   After drastic alterations in 1969-70, there was only one through platform (centre) and one bay (right). This 1976 panorama includes the former cattle dock (left), which was subsequently used by the engineers. (D.K.Jones coll.)

68.   An Aberdare to Cardiff DMU departs on the reversible running line on 9th August 1998. The junction can be seen at the far end of the extensive roof. On the left are the former relief lines. Note the changes at street level, where a new entrance was completed in 1976. The signal box is near the junction and it closed on 15th October 1998. (D.H.Mitchell)

69. The south end of the station was recorded on 11th October 1998, as no. 37671 *Tre Pol & Pen* worked a waste train. On the right is the final bay to have been taken out of use. It had been numbered 7. (M.J.Stretton)

> **Other pictures of this station and details of the junction move are in our first volume on the area, *Pontypridd to Port Talbot*.**

70. Bound for Barry Island on 13th February 2009 is Pacer no. 142072. The white structure beyond it is a new platform, which was opened on 16th September 1991, as traffic was increasing. It was subsequently lengthened from four to six-car capacity. (V.Mitchell)

2. To Taff Vale from Wenvoe
WENVOE

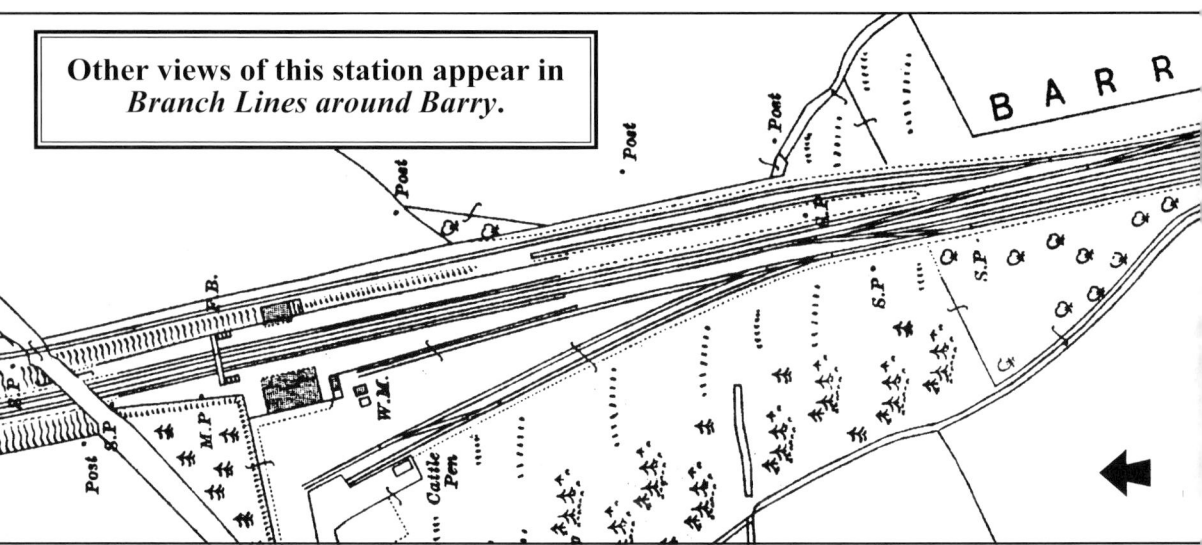

Other views of this station appear in *Branch Lines around Barry*.

XVIII. This 1920 extract has double track passing under a bridge on the left, with a single line on a level crossing. This track continued north to Alps Quarry. A siding to a reservoir is the lower line on the right and above it are the running lines, flanked by loops. The good yard closed on 2nd December 1963.

71. This southward view was recorded soon after the 1963 closure of the route. The 31-lever signal box was in the far distance and was probably switched out.
(Lens of Sutton coll.)

72. The main building is seen in 1983, in use as a dwelling. To the north was Wenvoe Tunnel which was 1868yds in length. The provisions were generous for a population of less than 500. (D.K.Jones coll.)

NORTH OF WENVOE

73.   This location can be found on map II, in the lower left corner of the right page. No. 5046 *Earl Cawdor*, a "Castle" class 4-6-0, is hauling a van train from Swansea to Cardiff on 30th September 1957. The viaduct in the background was built by the Barry Railway, over the GWR; the other structures carry a lane. (D.K.Jones coll.)

74.   The single line curve carried a few peak hour trains until its closure on 10th September 1962. No. 6438 is on Tynycaeau Spur with a Cardiff Clarence Road to Pontypridd service on 2nd May 1959. North of the junction was St Y Nyll Platform, but it was only open from July to November of 1905. (S.C.L.Philips/D.K.Jones coll.)

CREIGIAU

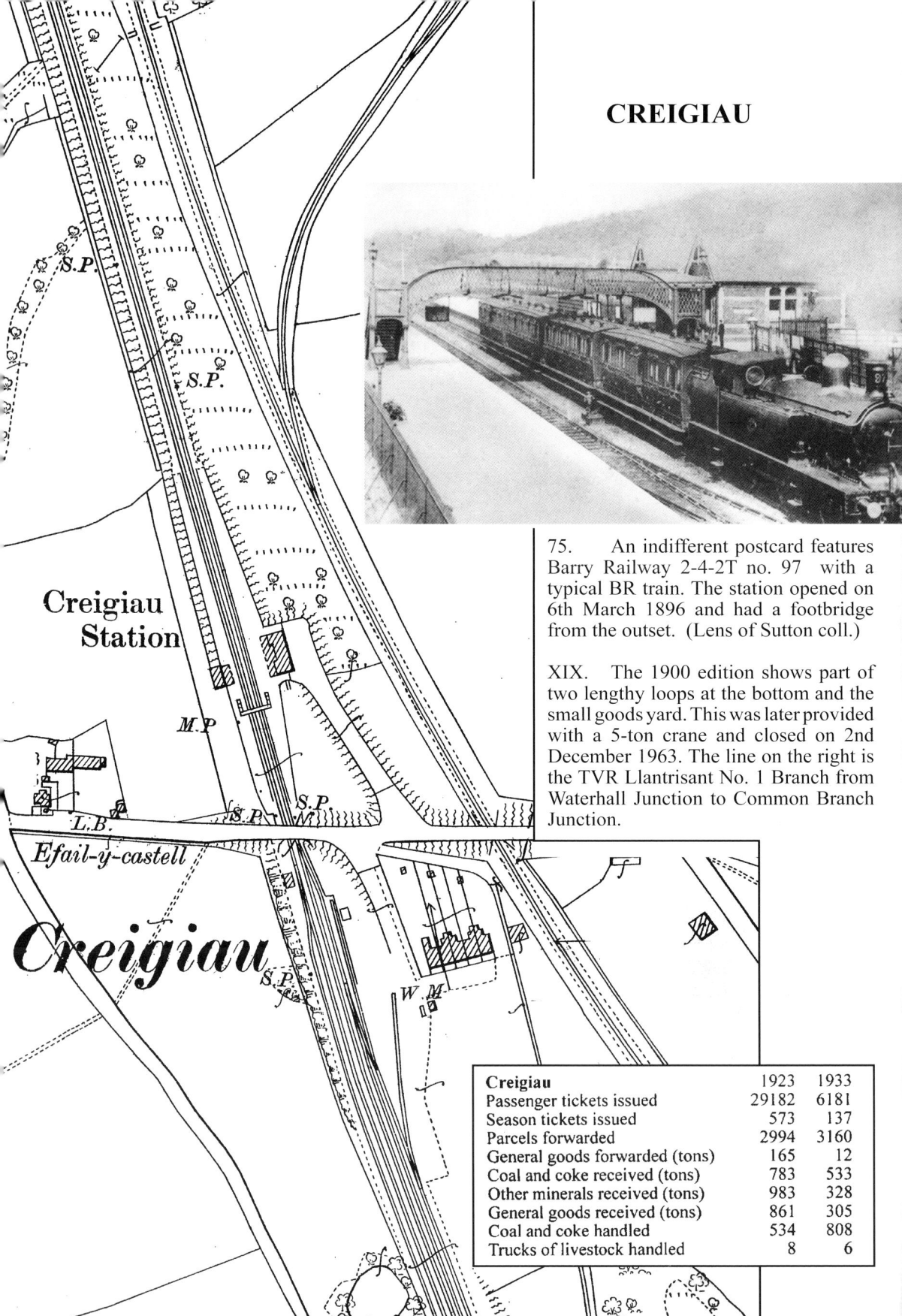

75.   An indifferent postcard features Barry Railway 2-4-2T no. 97 with a typical BR train. The station opened on 6th March 1896 and had a footbridge from the outset. (Lens of Sutton coll.)

XIX.   The 1900 edition shows part of two lengthy loops at the bottom and the small goods yard. This was later provided with a 5-ton crane and closed on 2nd December 1963. The line on the right is the TVR Llantrisant No. 1 Branch from Waterhall Junction to Common Branch Junction.

Creigiau Station

Efail-y-castell

Creigiau

Creigiau	1923	1933
Passenger tickets issued	29182	6181
Season tickets issued	573	137
Parcels forwarded	2994	3160
General goods forwarded (tons)	165	12
Coal and coke received (tons)	783	533
Other minerals received (tons)	983	328
General goods received (tons)	861	305
Coal and coke handled	534	808
Trucks of livestock handled	8	6

76. The long arms of the BR signals can be discerned, as can the loops and associated sidings. The BR made generous provision at several stations to accommodate coal trains waiting for ships.
(Lens of Sutton coll.)

77. The 25-lever signal box was south of the road bridge and was photographed on 3rd September 1954. There were three private sidings listed in 1938. The staff dropped here from 21 in 1923 to 7 in 1932.
(S.Rickard/J&J coll.)

78. Seen on the same day is the 9.55am Creigiau to Cardiff Clarence Road auto train, headed by 2-6-2T no. 5529. Notice that the signal arms are shorter and that two loops are signalled.
(S.Rickard/J&J coll.)

79.   Calling at the well kept station on 9th September 1960 is 0-6-0PT no. 6438 with the 5.31pm Cardiff Clarence Road to Pontypridd service. Passenger trains were withdrawn on 10th September 1962. (S.Rickard/J&J coll.)

80.   The Monmouthshire Railway Society visited Creigiau Quarry on 26th March 1977. The "Cardiff Valleys" left Newport at 10.50 and also visited Penarth Curve North, Taffs Well, Aber Junction, Nelson, Dowlais, Bute Road, Llantrisant, Coed Ely and Cwm Colliery. (R.A.Lumber/D.H.Mitchell)

EFAIL ISAF

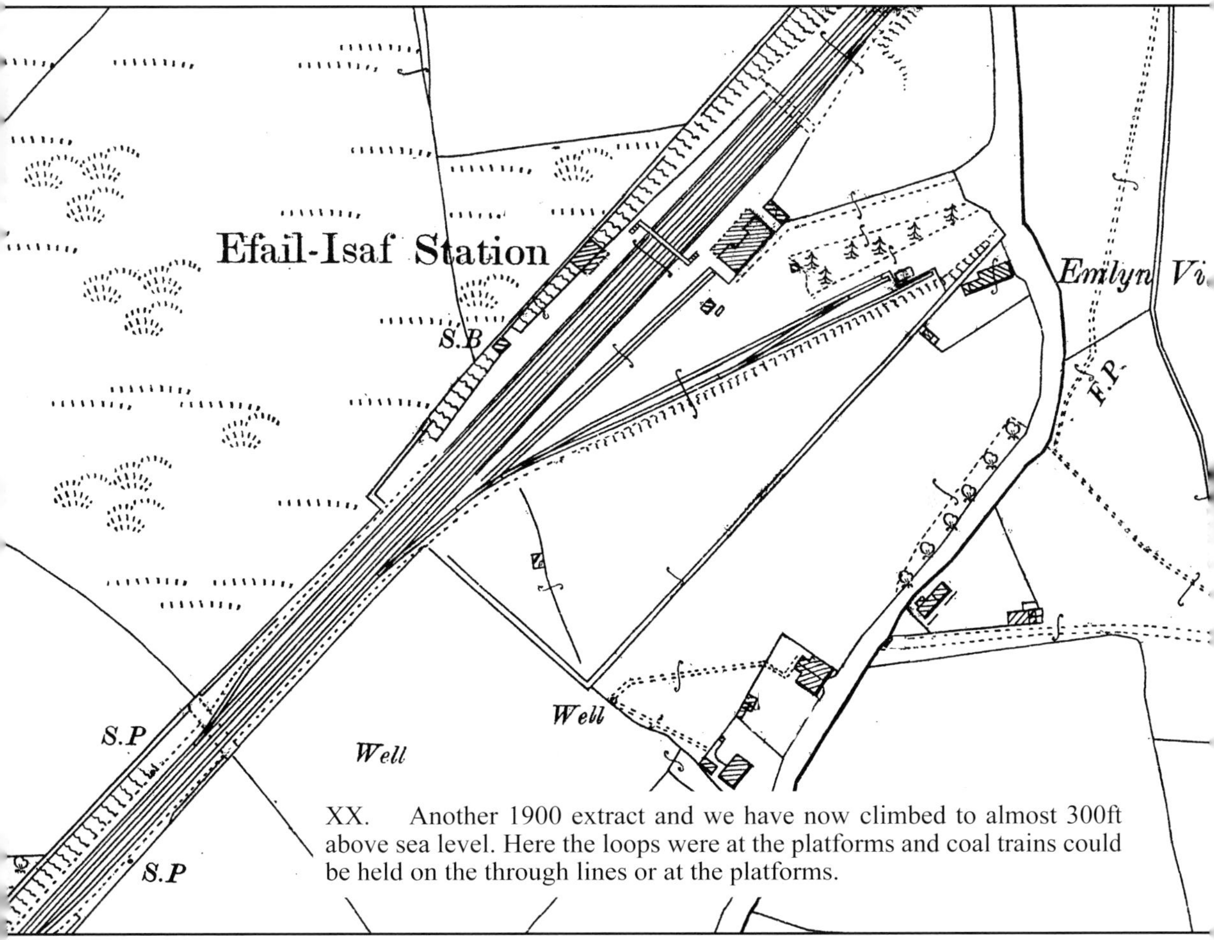

Efail-Isaf Station

S.B.

Emlyn Vi.

F.P.

S.P.

Well

Well

S.P.

XX.   Another 1900 extract and we have now climbed to almost 300ft above sea level. Here the loops were at the platforms and coal trains could be held on the through lines or at the platforms.

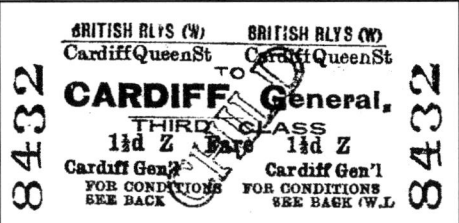

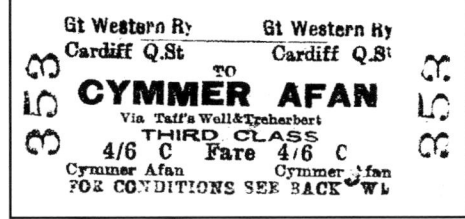

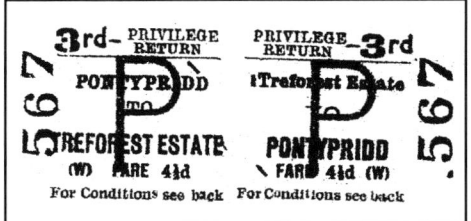

81.   The station opened on 6th March 1896 and demanded a double length footbridge for the small number of passengers. The 28-lever signal box is out of view, but some of the men are included. There were 13 in 1923 and 4 in 1936. (Lens of Sutton coll.)

82.   The train seen in picture 79 was recorded here, thanks to a cooperative guard and thus we can enjoy a direct comparison between the two stations. This one lost both its passenger and goods services on 10th September 1962. (S.Rickard/J&J coll.)

TONTEG HALT

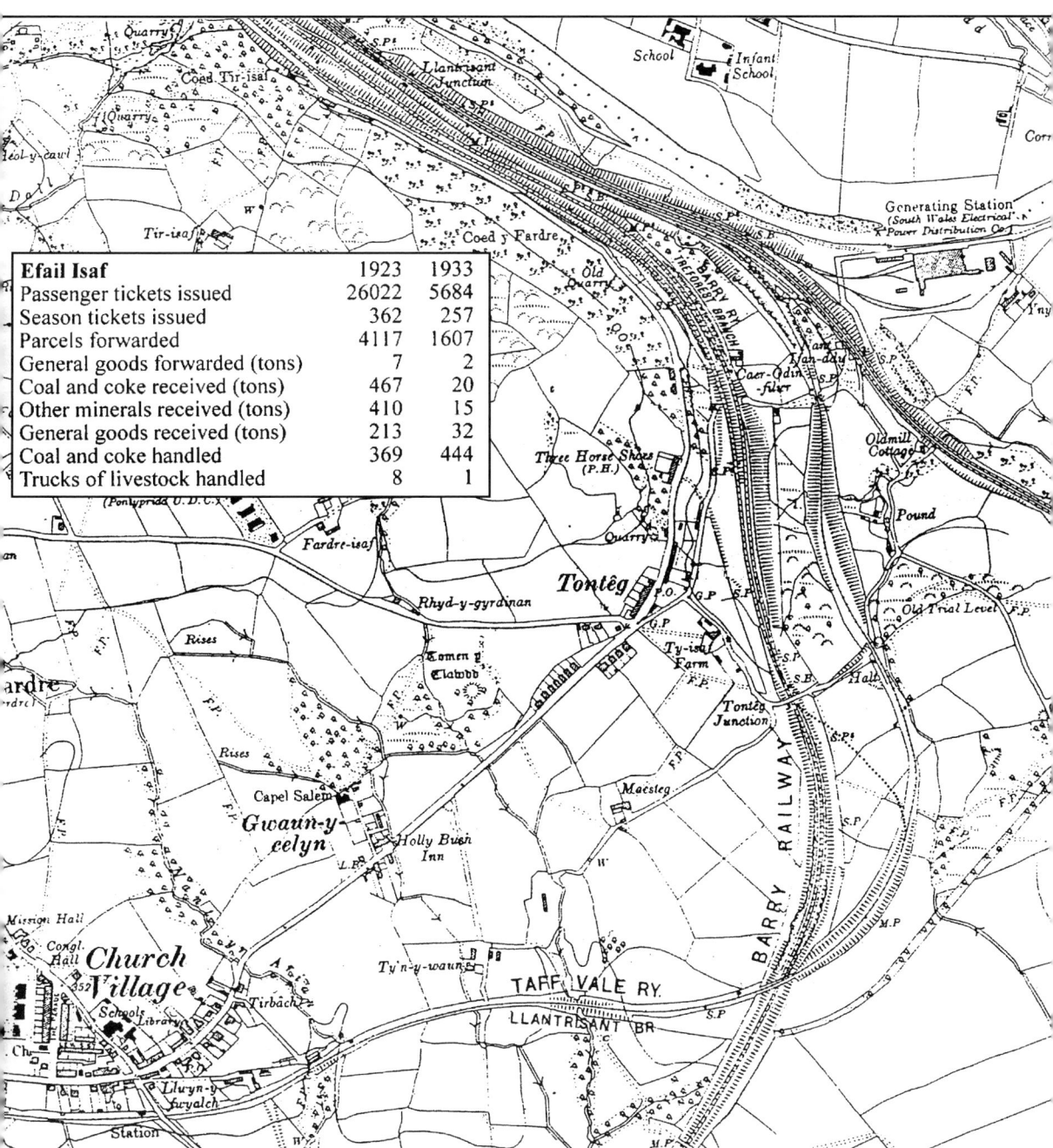

Efail Isaf	1923	1933
Passenger tickets issued	26022	5684
Season tickets issued	362	257
Parcels forwarded	4117	1607
General goods forwarded (tons)	7	2
Coal and coke received (tons)	467	20
Other minerals received (tons)	410	15
General goods received (tons)	213	32
Coal and coke handled	369	444
Trucks of livestock handled	8	1

XXI.   One halt is shown on the 1921 edition at 6ins to 1 mile, it serving one farm, one public house and about 30 dwellings. A dotted line shows how the GWR rearranged the connections in 1930.

83.   There were two halts close by one another until 1962. They were nearer the village than the first and close to the northern end of the 1930 connection. Running on the former Barry Railway route from Llantrisant to Pontypridd (Coke Ovens) on 25th October 1956 is 0-6-2T no. 5699. (S.Rickard/J&J coll.)

84.   Another 5600 class 0-6-2T was recorded on the same day running in the other direction. Pity about the low light. (S.Rickard/J&J coll.)

85.   A third view from the same bridge that day has 0-6-2T no. 5680 hauling coal from Cwm Colliery to Maritime Colliery. The disused former Barry main line is on the left, it continuing to Hafod Junction. (S.Rickard/J&J coll.)

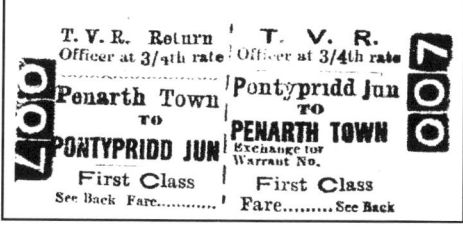

86. Our survey finishes with two views from 2nd May 1959 of Treforest Junction. No. 6438 approaches the halt from the south, working from Clarence Road to Pontypridd. (S.C.L.Philips/ D.K.Jones coll.)

87. The Llantrisant branch is on the left as we depart north and look back at the halt. The signal box closed on 28th September 1964 and had 46 levers. The halt for Llantrisant trains closed in 1952 and the other in 1962. (S.C.L.Philips/ D.K.Jones coll.)

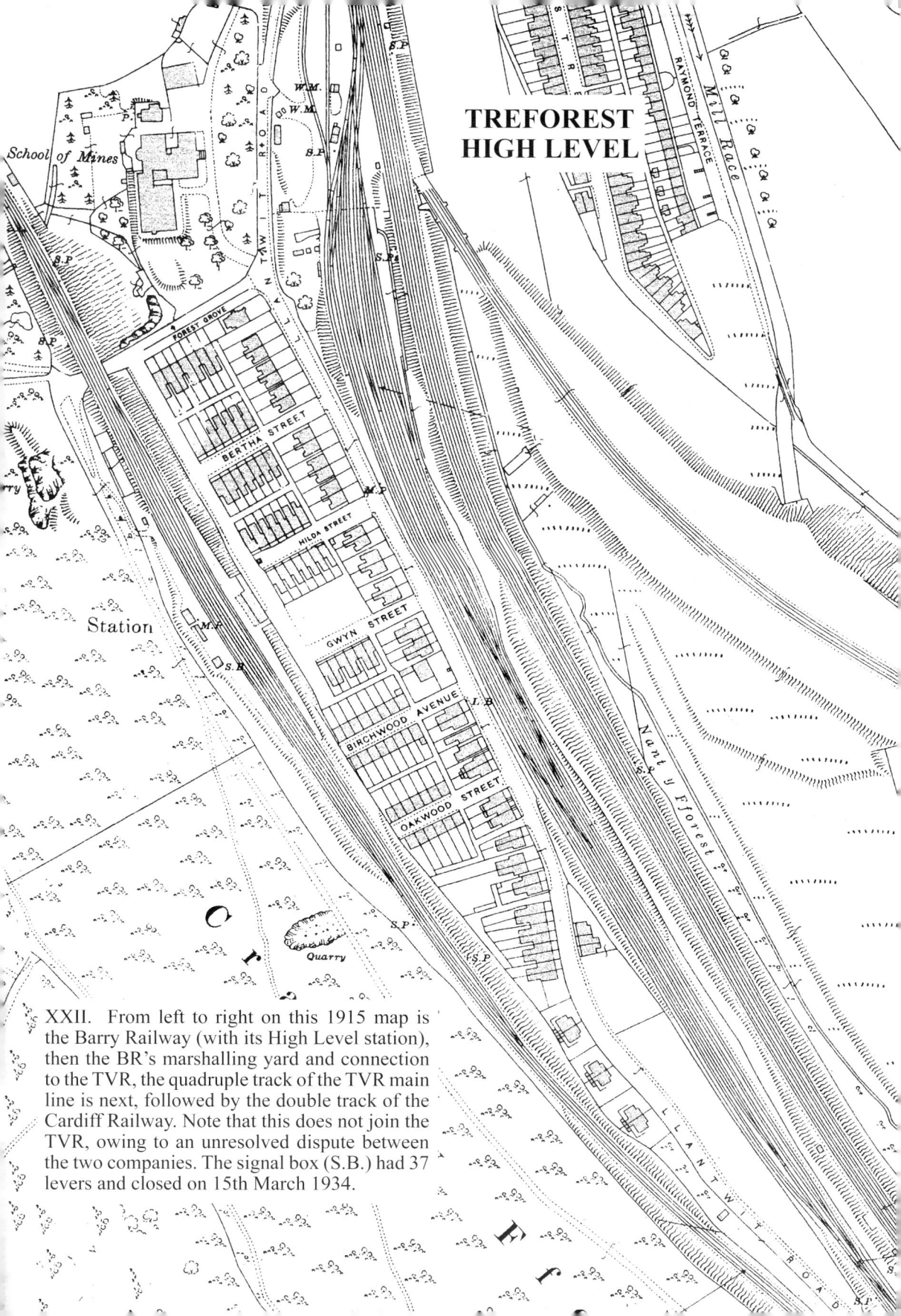

TREFOREST HIGH LEVEL

School of Mines

Station

Quarry

XXII. From left to right on this 1915 map is the Barry Railway (with its High Level station), then the BR's marshalling yard and connection to the TVR, the quadruple track of the TVR main line is next, followed by the double track of the Cardiff Railway. Note that this does not join the TVR, owing to an unresolved dispute between the two companies. The signal box (S.B.) had 37 levers and closed on 15th March 1934.

88.　This station opened later than its neighbours on 1st April 1898 and it had four tracks with a long footbridge, as at Efail Isaf. The view is from April 1958; the route was in use for through freight traffic until 1951. (M.Hale)

89.　The prospective passenger's perspective was impressive indeed, even as late as the 1950s. The nearer part was added in 1908 and contained a new booking office. Known as High Level from 1st July 1924, the station was open to passengers until 5th May 1930. Llantwit Road Yard handled the goods traffic until 1st September 1930. (A.Dudman coll.)

PONTYPRIDD GRAIG

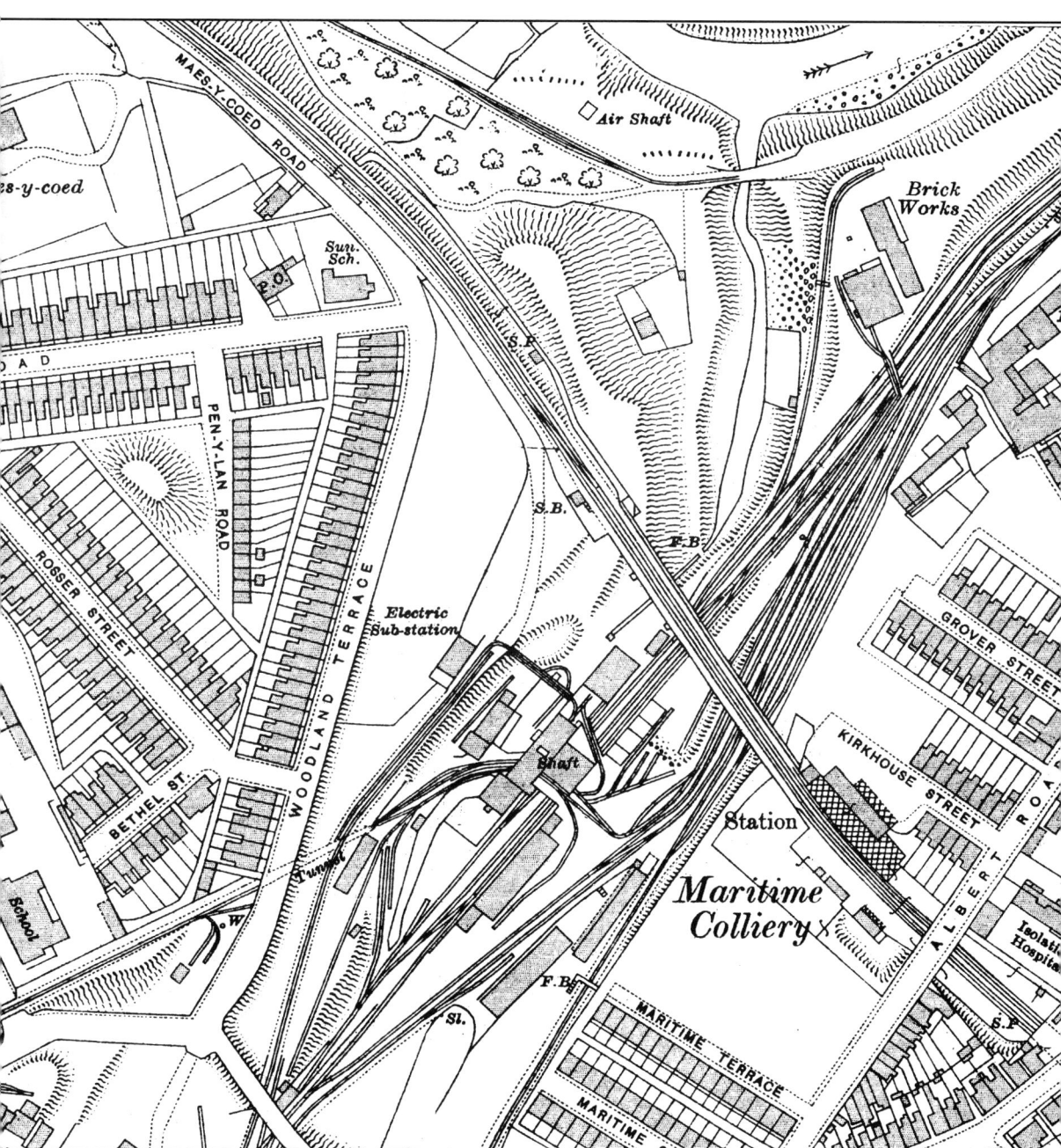

XXIIIa. The station is above the words "Maritime Colliery" and the squared pattern represents the extent of the glazed canopies. The 1919 edition is a continuation of map XVII, but only the colliery tracks appear on both. The signal box is near the centre. It had a 21-lever frame and had closed in 1907.

90.   The frontage is seen from Kirkhouse Street not long after the station opened on 16th March 1896. The word "Graig" was added by the GWR on 1st July 1924. There was a staff of 16 that year. (Lens of Sutton coll.)

91.   The bridge for Albert Road is centre and evidence of the subway can be found on the left of this 1922 view, when only one track was in use. The tunnel length was 1323yds and it was subject to subsidence, with resultant track closure on one side. (D.K.Jones coll.)

92.   A northward view in July 1958 shows the main building surrounded by commercial extensions. Centre are the abutments of the bridge over the colliery lines, the spans of which had been removed a few months earlier. (D.K.Jones coll.)

NORTH OF PONTYPRIDD GRAIG

XXIIIb. The BR goods yard is centre on this 1919 survey at 15ins to 1 mile and the TVR Rhondda Valley line is upper right.

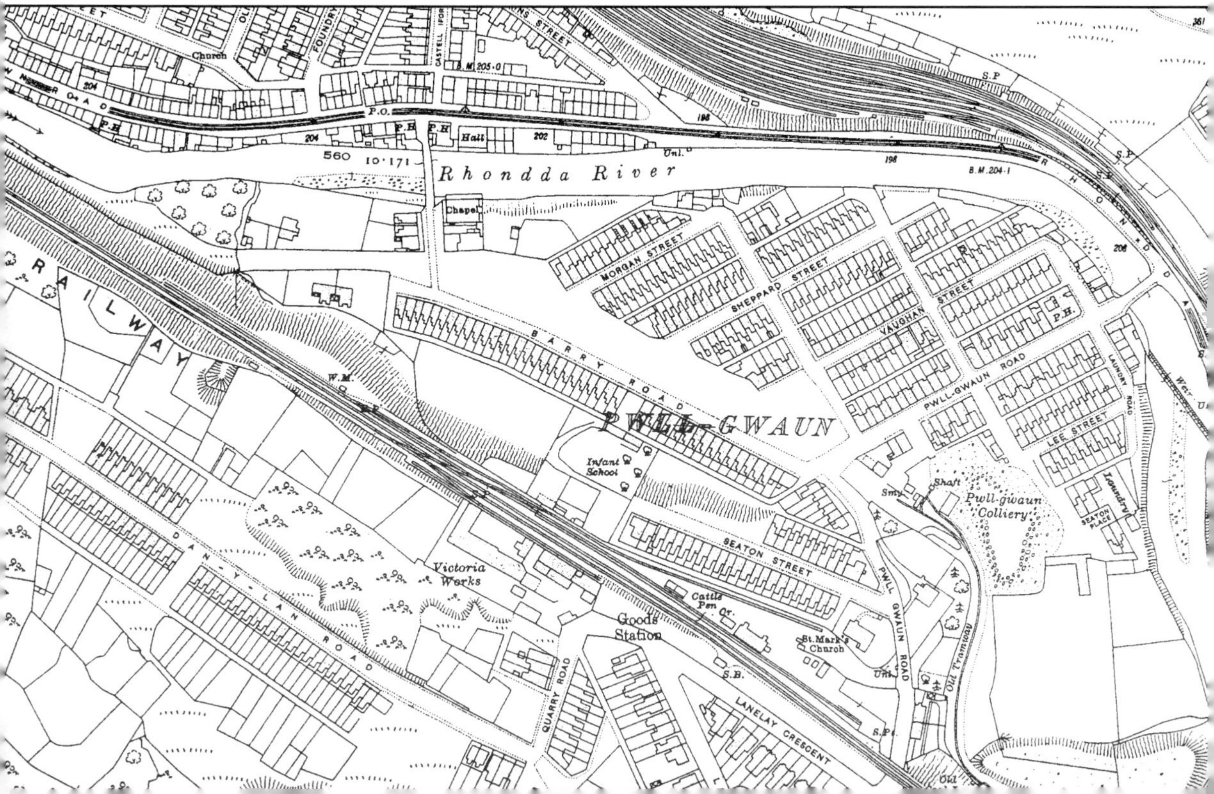

3. To Taff Vale from Llantrisant
LLANTRISANT

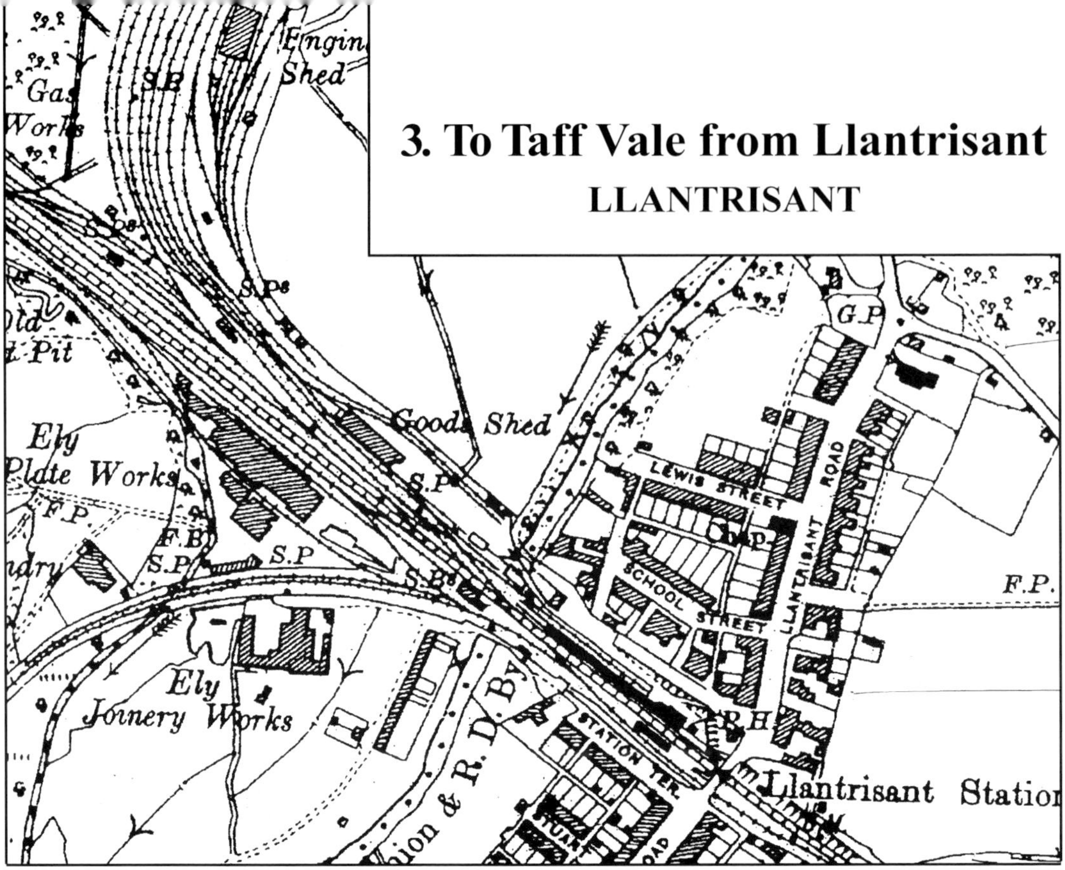

XXIV. We will travel north, using a curve close to the engine shed (top left). Reference to map II (left page) shows that we will soon turn east (at Mwyndy Junction) and pass north of Llantrisant, which is more than a mile from its station. The GWR main line is diagonally across this 1921 extract at 12ins to 1 mile. The curve on the left is the Cowbridge branch, which opened in 1865, lost its passenger trains in 1951 and closed in 1965.

93. We look east on a postcard showing the station at its optimum. The bay platform on the left was used by trains to Pontypridd and to Penygraig, the latter until June 1958. Prior to 1922, most TVR trains used the platform on the right. (Lens of Sutton coll.)

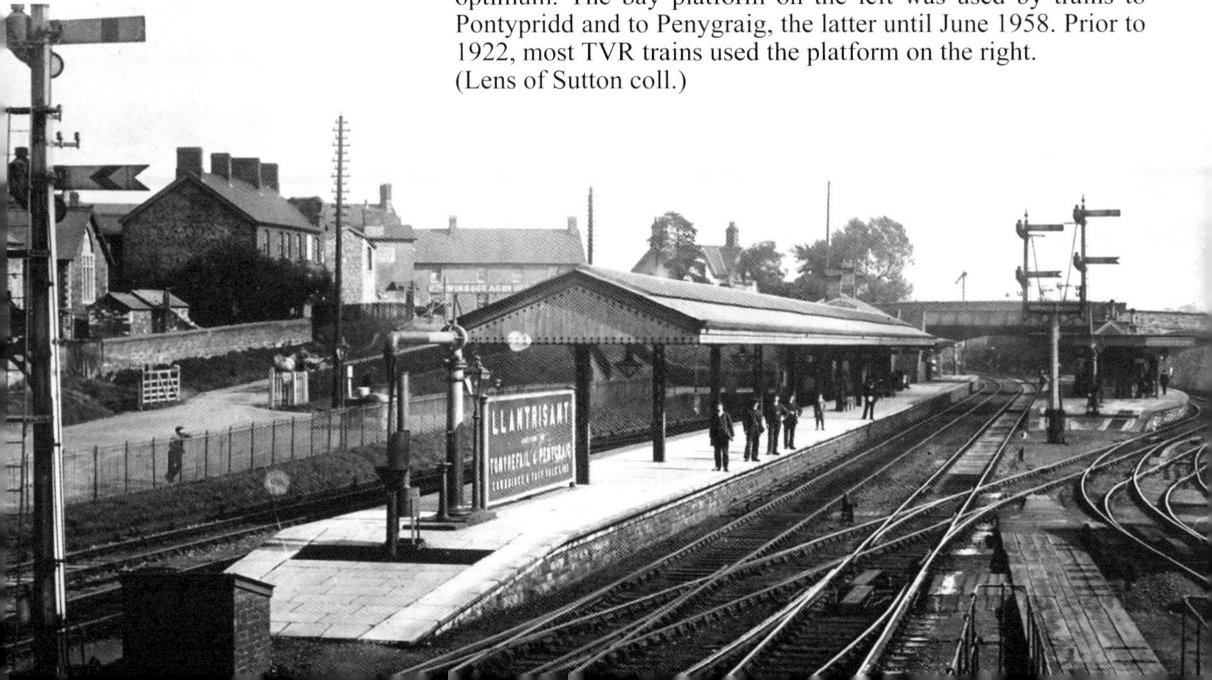

94.   A westward panorama in May 1951 has the Cowbridge branch curving to the left and the goods shed in the right distance. The large building to the left of the main line is the Ely Tin Plate Works, which had its own siding. (P.J.Garland/R.S.Carpenter)

95.   The engine shed housed 15 locomotives at its busiest time and its final BR coding was 88G. It is seen on 5th May 1951 with nos. 1421, 4620 and 3776 in attendance. (H.C.Casserley)

Other views of Llantrisant can be found in our *Cardiff to Swansea* album.

96.   The water column appears also in the previous photograph. It was supplied from the tank above the coal stage, which was filled with water pumped from the nearby River Ely. The photograph is from the 1930s. (R.S.Carpenter coll.)

97.   Leaving for Penygraig on 13th July 1957 is 0-6-0PT no. 4674. The distant signal has no spectacles, as it is fixed. The diesel depot closed on 27th March 1987, as coal traffic had declined. (S.Rickard/J&J coll.)

98. Seen on 3rd May 1958 is 0-4-2T no. 1471, with a vast number of open telephone wires above its chimney. This was the original SWR platform and has early rivetted stanchions. The station closed on 2nd November 1964 and reopened as Pontyclun on 28th September 1992. (G.Adams/M.J.Stretton coll.)

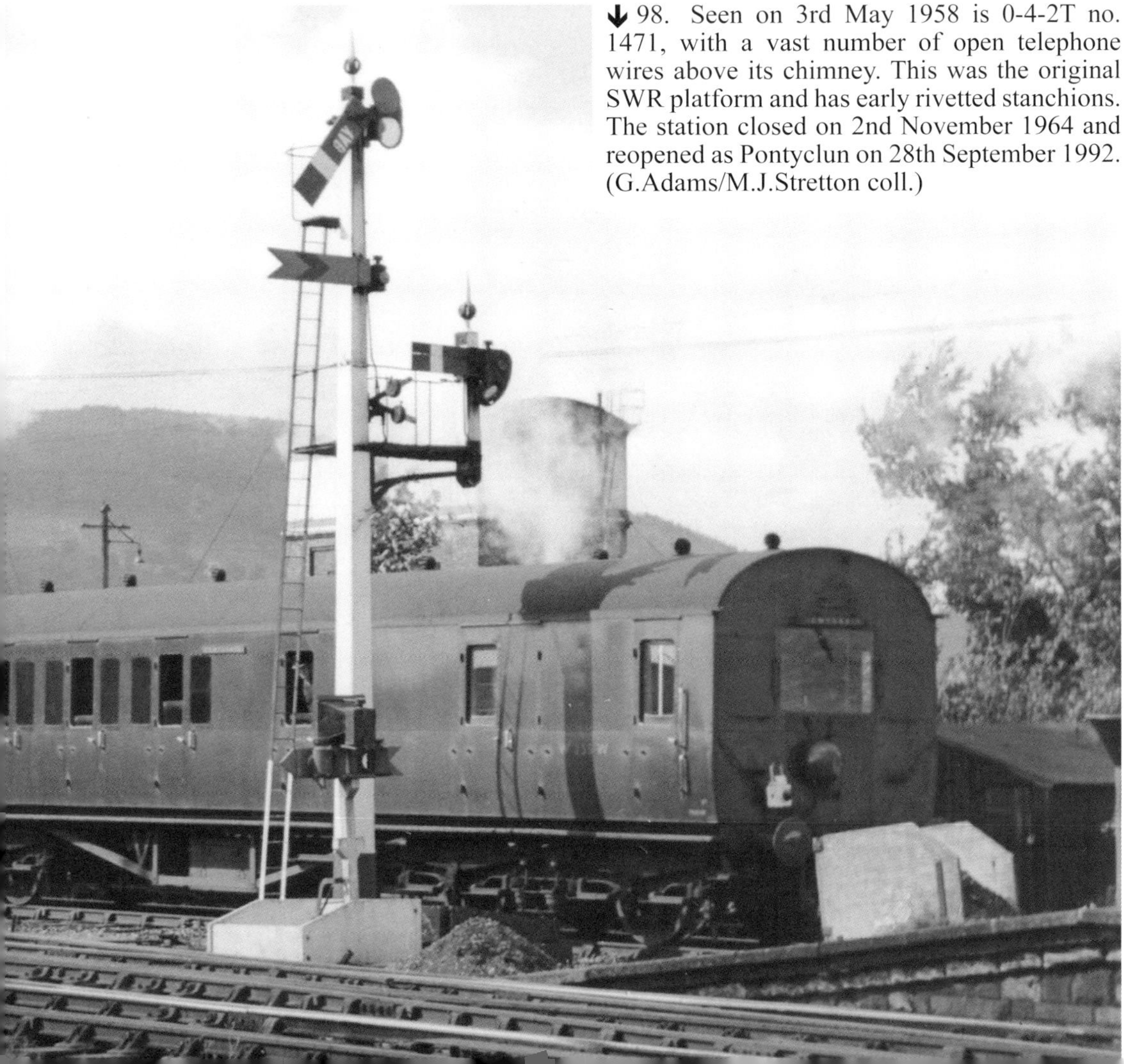

CROSS INN

XXV.   This was the nearest station to Llantrisant and is near the lower border of this extract from the 1921 edition at 6ins to 1 mile. Further south was the mineral line to Mwyndy and Brofiscen, which can be found on map II. Our route is on the right and it soon reaches Beddau Halt, which opened in 1910. At the top is the Llantrisant Common branch. The fences near the curve on it once flanked the line to Gelynog Colliery. There had been an engine shed at the east end of the triangle until 1904.

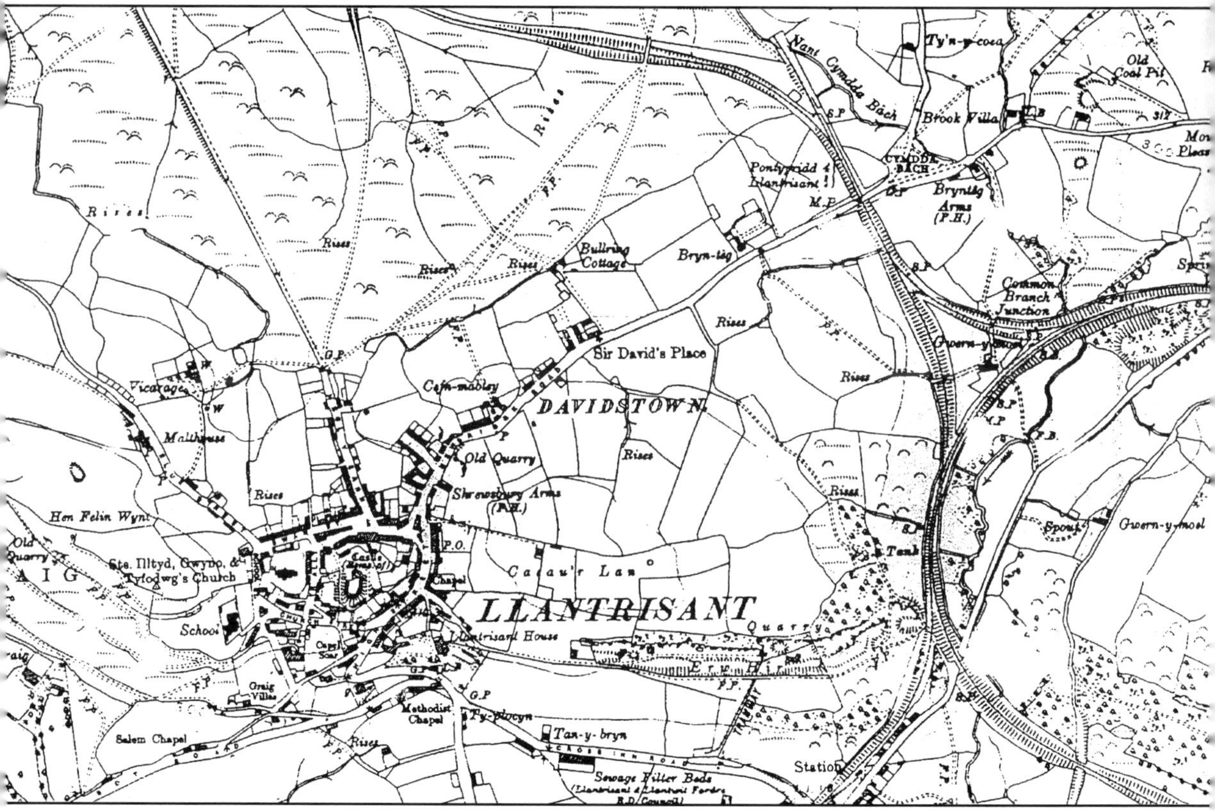

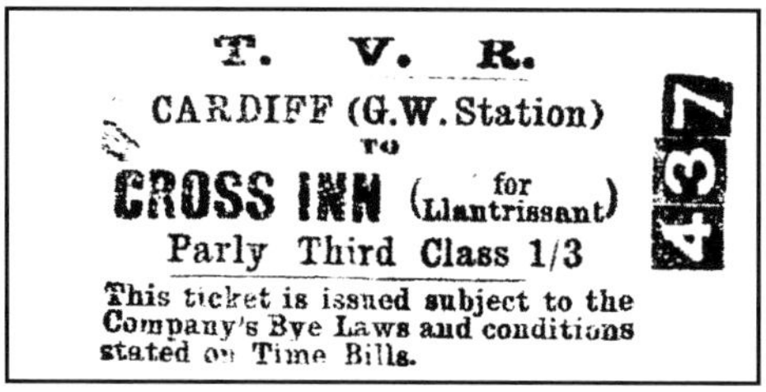

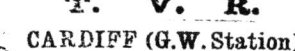

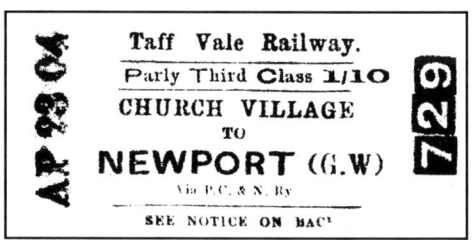

Cross Inn	1923	1933
Passenger tickets issued	30578	4628
Season tickets issued	232	113
Parcels forwarded	8974	5860
General goods forwarded (tons)	1447	20
Coal and coke received (tons)	714	39
Other minerals received (tons)	4341	908
General goods received (tons)	1848	293
Coal and coke handled	2215	1003
Trucks of livestock handled	11	7

99.   The station is seen from the north on 15th July 1959, with the small goods shed beyond. Goods traffic had ceased on 30th August 1953. There were ten men here for most of the 1930s. (R.M.Casserley)

XXVI. The 1899 survey does not include the small signal box, which had closed in 1895.

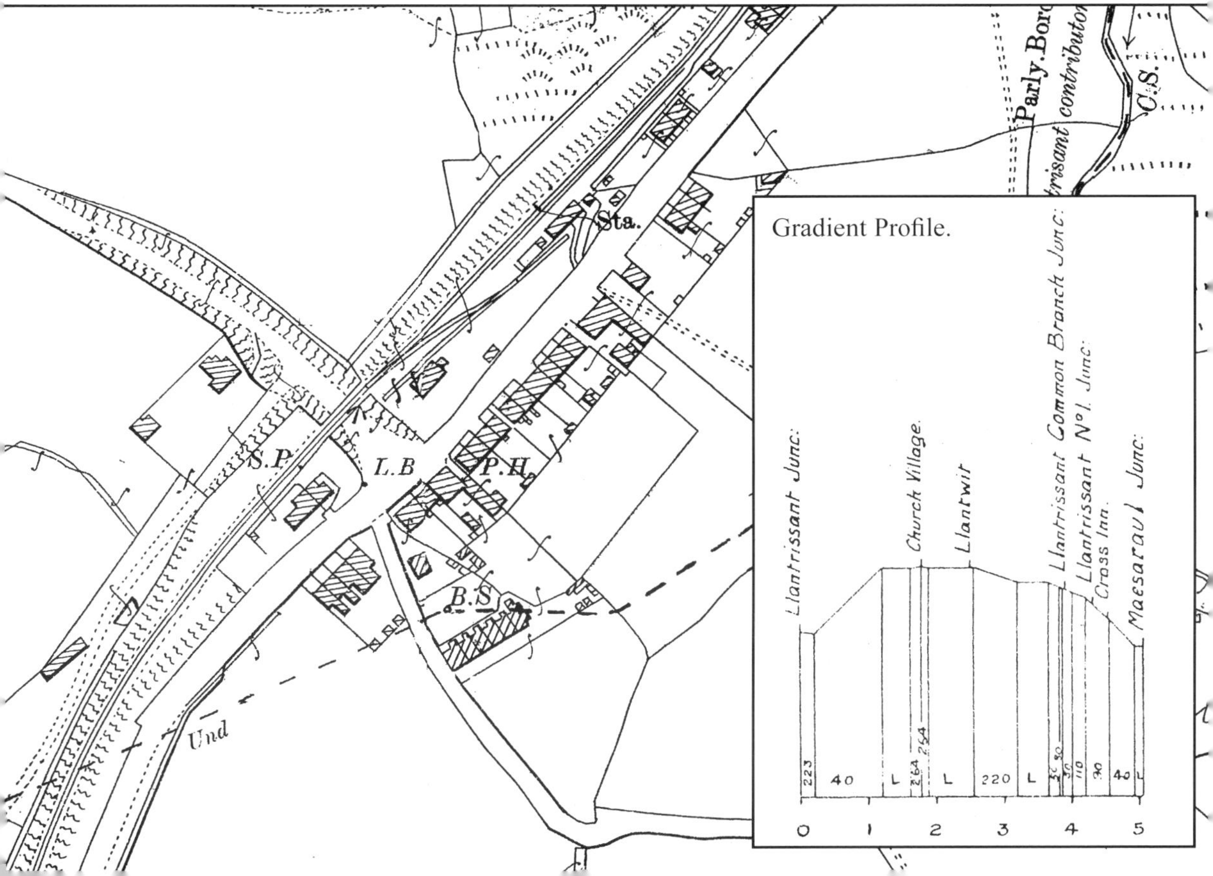

LLANTWIT FARDRE

Llantwit Fardre	1923	1933
Passenger tickets issued	24351	1138
Season tickets issued	284	154
Parcels forwarded	4320	9149
General goods forwarded (tons)	348	171
Coal and coke received (tons)	233	400
Other minerals received (tons)	6286	1100
General goods received (tons)	13786	12420
Coal and coke handled	205246	415791
Trucks of livestock handled	11	4

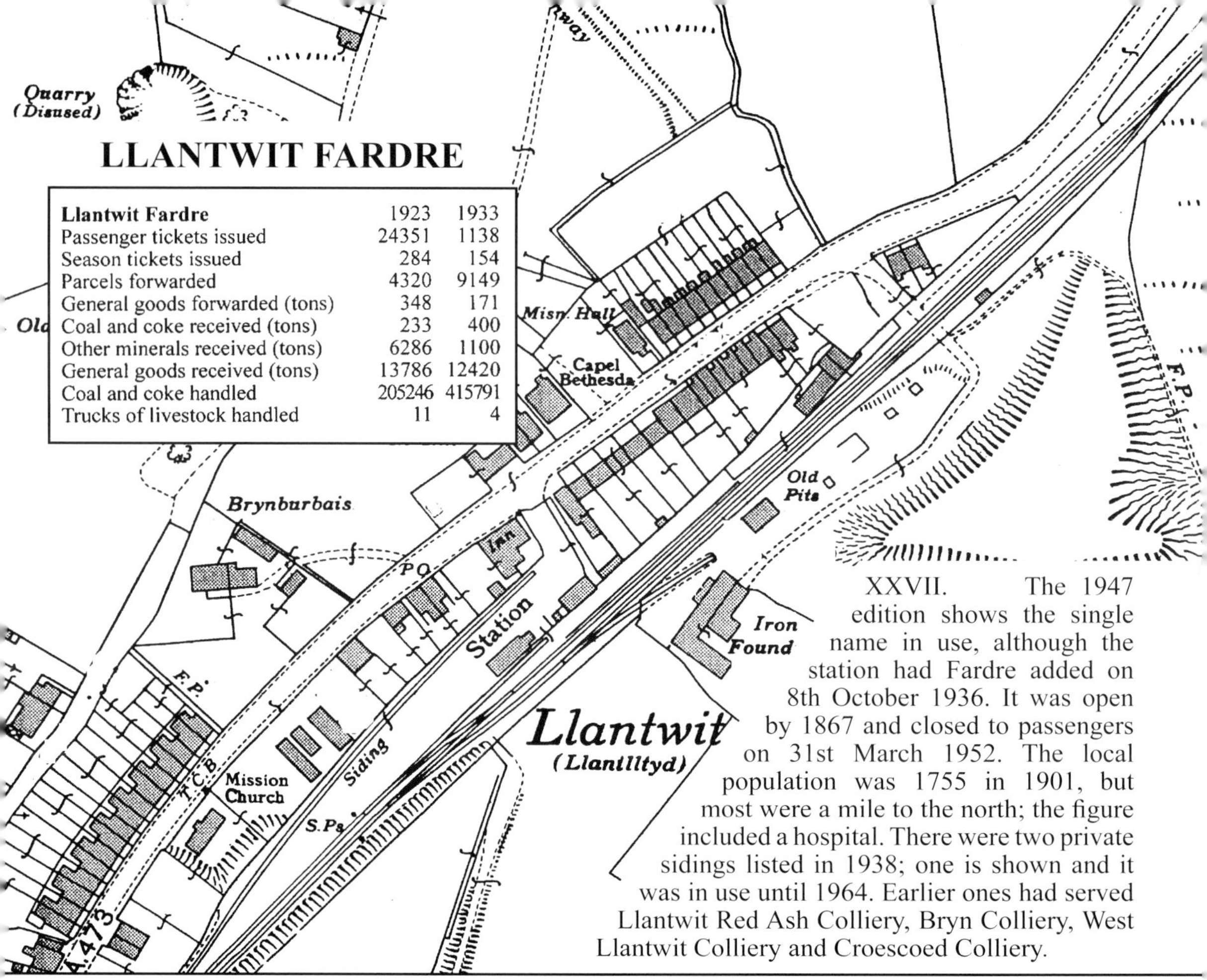

XXVII. The 1947 edition shows the single name in use, although the station had Fardre added on 8th October 1936. It was open by 1867 and closed to passengers on 31st March 1952. The local population was 1755 in 1901, but most were a mile to the north; the figure included a hospital. There were two private sidings listed in 1938; one is shown and it was in use until 1964. Earlier ones had served Llantwit Red Ash Colliery, Bryn Colliery, West Llantwit Colliery and Croescoed Colliery.

100.   A 1954 photograph gives a good impression of the building, which lasted into the 1960s. The signal box closed on 11th June 1957 and the goods yard followed on 7th October 1963. The foundry private siding is on the right. There was a 20-lever signal box until 11th June 1957. The staff dropped from 10 in 1923 to 7 in 1936. (H.C.Casserley)

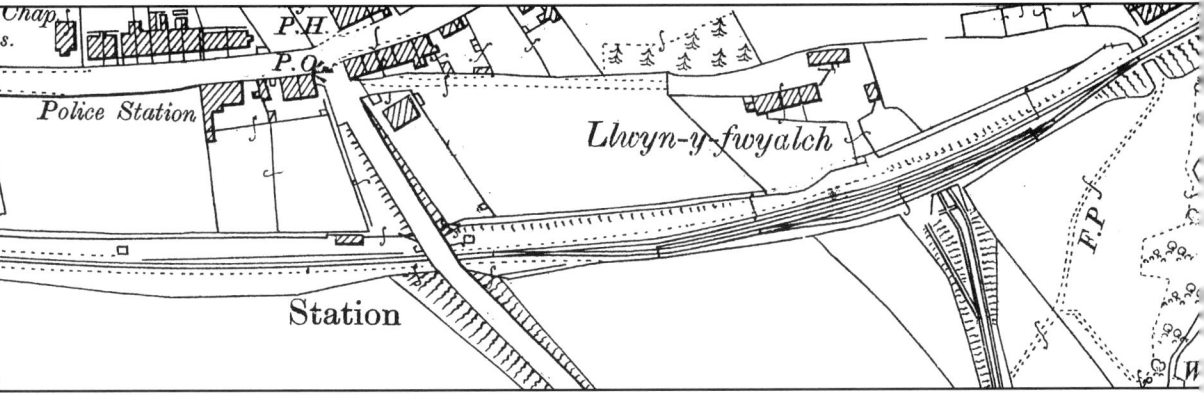

XXVIII. The 1900 revision includes a tramway south to Taff Llantwit Colliery (1890-1903). The passenger platform is to the left of the road bridge.

101.   The station opened on 1st October 1887 and the platform was extended in 1892. This was usually the busiest station on the branch. (Lens of Sutton coll.)

102.   Local enterprise took over the premises, which were photographed in July 1959. Fame came to the village when Gilbern cars were built there, as the firm was recorded as the only motor manufacturer in Wales. A fine sports saloon was made in 1961-1969, the name being a corruption of the partners Christian names. (R.M.Casserley)

4. To Taff Vale from Caerphilly

XXIX. Our journey in this section is over the route marked Alexandra Docks Railway. Its full name and name changes are given in the introduction. The location of the first station at Caerphilly is shown, this lasting until the RR opened its direct route to Cardiff. The diagram is pre-1922.

CAERPHILLY

> **Other views of the area can be seen in our *Cardiff to Dowlais* album.**

103. Four tracks through the station date from 1913 and are seen from the west in about 1935. A bay platform was also added in 1913, but there were only two through platforms again from 1973. (Stations UK)

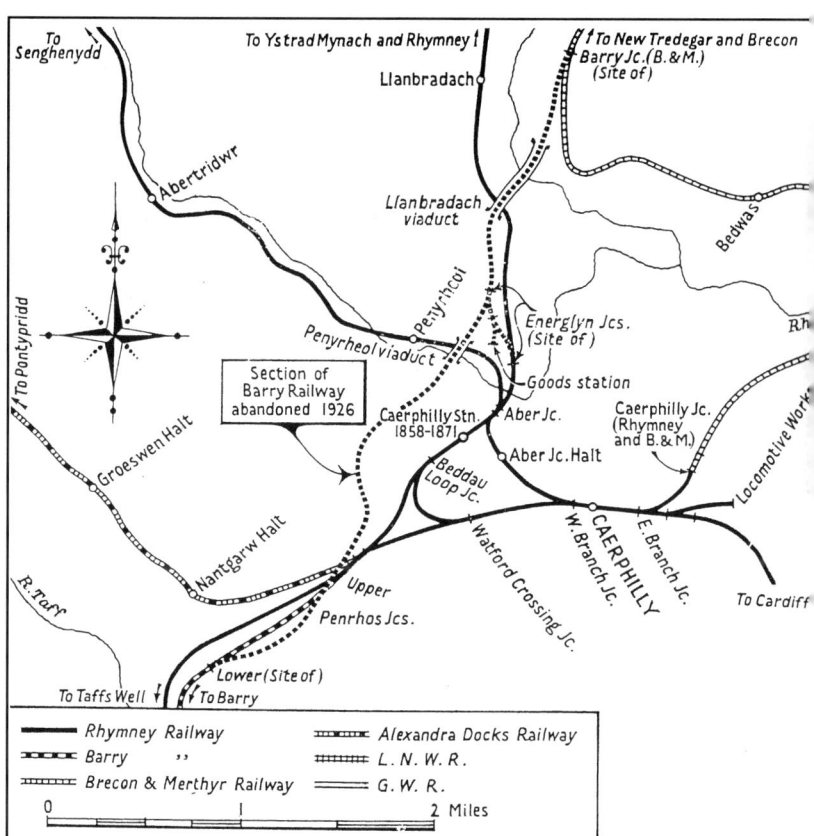

To Senghenydd

To Ystrad Mynach and Rhymney ↑

↑ To New Tredegar and Brecon
Barry Jc. (B. & M.)
(Site of)

Llanbradach

Abertridwr

Llanbradach viaduct

Bedwas

To Pontypridd

Penyrheol

Penyrheol viaduct

Energlyn Jcs.
(Site of)

Rh...

Section of
Barry Railway
abandoned 1926

Goods station

Groeswen Halt

Caerphilly Stn.
1858-1871

Aber Jc.

Caerphilly Jc.
(Rhymney
and B.& M.)

Locomotive Works

Aber Jc. Halt

Beddau
Loop Jc.

Nantgarw Halt

Watford Crossing Jc.

W. Branch Jc.

CAERPHILLY

E. Branch Jc.

To Cardiff

R. Taff

Upper
Penrhos Jcs.

Lower (Site of)

To Taffs Well ↑   ↑ To Barry

━━━━	Rhymney Railway	▨▨▨▨	Alexandra Docks Railway
✕✕✕✕	Barry ,,	▥▥▥▥	L. N. W. R.
▥▥▥▥	Brecon & Merthyr Railway	══	G. W. R.

0   1   2 Miles

NANTGARW HALT HIGH LEVEL

104.   The 2.52pm Pontypridd to Machen was worked by 0-6-0PT no. 6411 on 4th September 1956, the last month of operation. The next three halts seem to have eluded our photographers. (S.Rickard/J&J coll.)

RHYDYFELIN HALT

105.   We look in a northwest direction in June 1922 as AD&R no. 14 approaches the basic halt. The 0-4-2T was ex-GWR no. 1426. The service was so successful that two coaches were often necessary at that period. The halt was moved ¼ mile south in 1928 and it closed on 2nd February 1953. The term High Level was added here on 1st July 1924. (D.K.Jones coll.)

TREFOREST HALT

← XXX. The 1921 map at 6ins to 1 mile reveals much industrial history and includes three halts and a station. Enjoy searching.

106. The date is 9th June 1952 and ground level access here was still necessary. The fencing had been added to keep passengers captive until the train arrived; the guard then unlocked the gate. The train is from Caerphilly. (T.B.Sands)

GLYNTAFF HALT

107. Seen on 31st July 1960, the site of the halt was beyond the girders of the road bridge in this northward view. The halt had closed on 5th May 1930. The signal box was called Interchange Sidings. (M.Hale)

TRAM ROAD HALT

XXXI. Pontypridd station is just beyond the left border of this map, which continues from no. XVII. The halt is near the centre and it was in use only until 10th July 1922, when Pontypridd became the northern terminus instead.

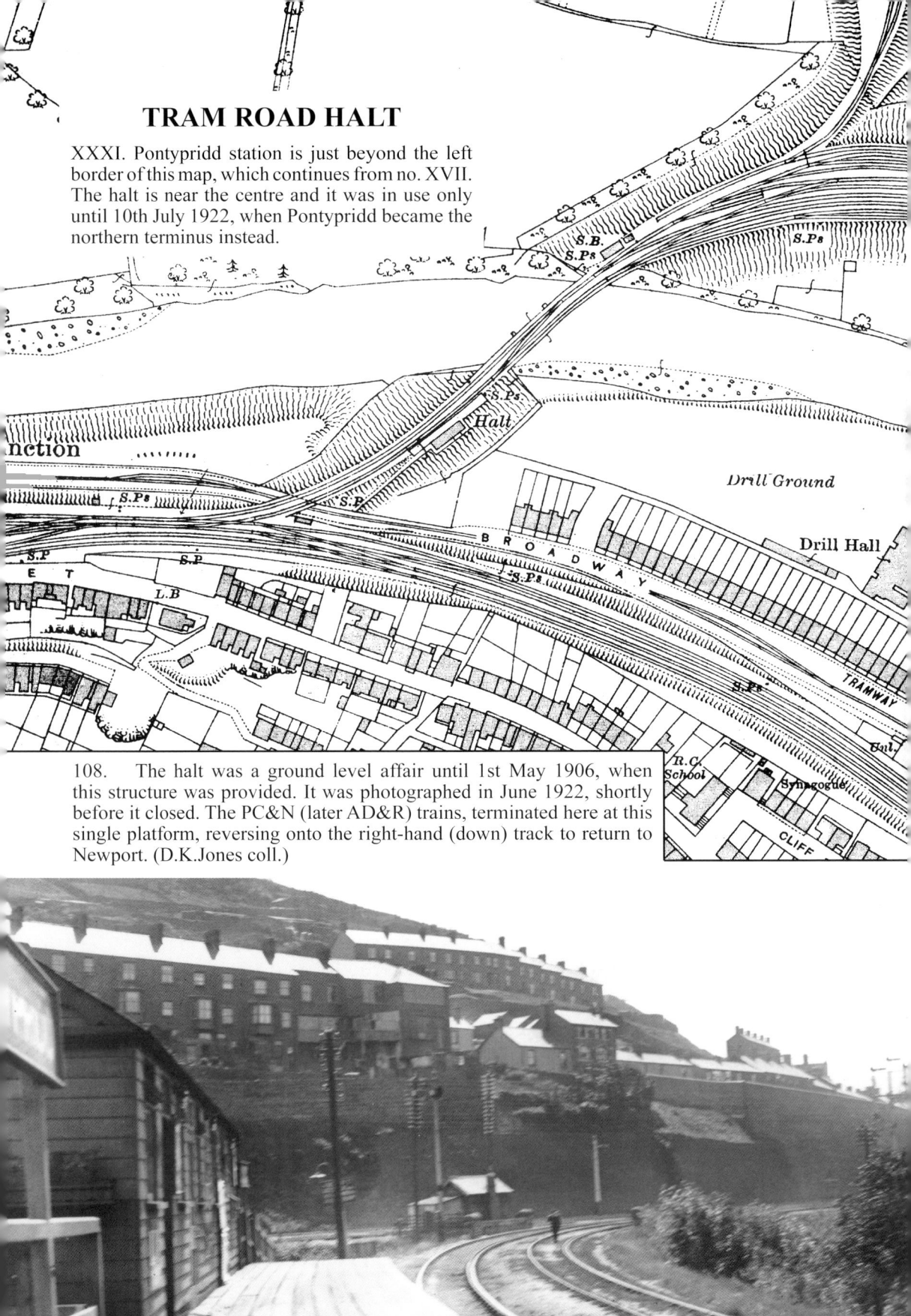

108.	The halt was a ground level affair until 1st May 1906, when this structure was provided. It was photographed in June 1922, shortly before it closed. The PC&N (later AD&R) trains, terminated here at this single platform, reversing onto the right-hand (down) track to return to Newport. (D.K.Jones coll.)

5. To Taff Vale from Coryton

CORYTON

109.   This became the passenger terminus of the former CR branch from Cardiff on 20th July 1931 and was still in use as such in 2011. An auto train is about to return to Cardiff sometime in the 1950s; the term Halt was used until 5th May 1969. The loop lasted until 15th October 1964. (Lens of Sutton coll.)

> **Other views of this station and the branch are included in our *Cardiff to Dowlais* album.**

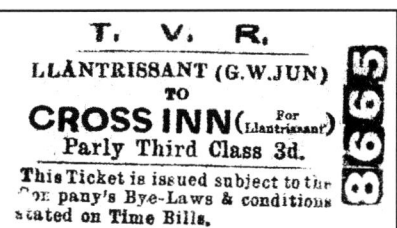

TONGWYNLAIS

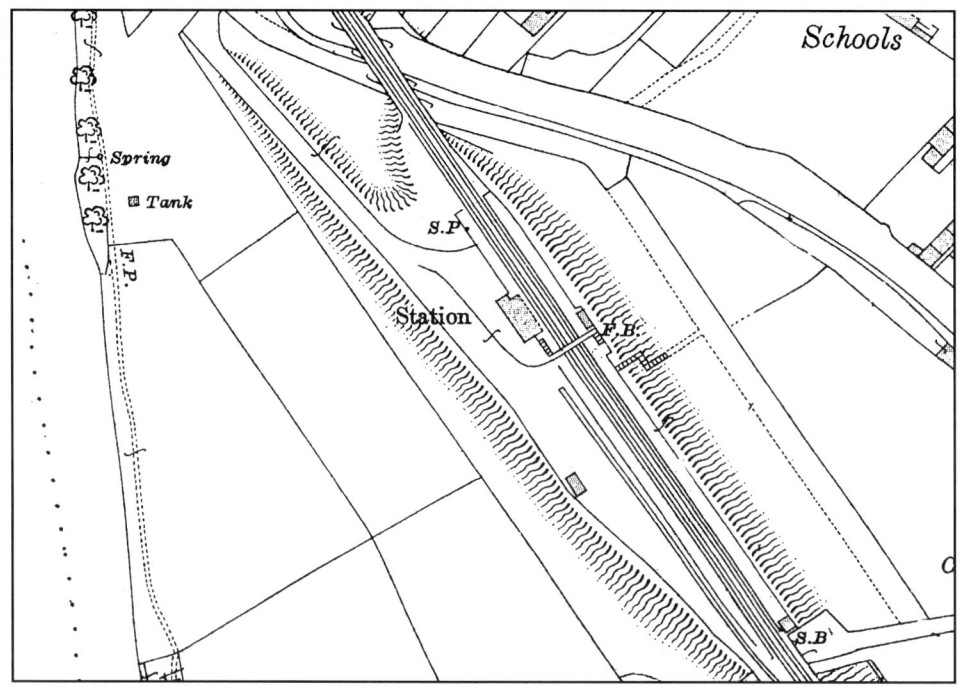

110.　The 1.05pm railmotor (No. 3) from Rhydyfelin, with driving trailer No. 4 leading, is approaching Tongwynlais Tunnel on 20th May 1919. (LCGB)

XXXIV. 1920 edition.

111. A southward view in August 1948 reveals the track still in place, optimistically. It was used again for coal traffic and construction materials for the new Nantgarw Colliery between 28th August 1951 and 16th June 1952. This was when the new connection to the ex-TVR route at Taffs Well was built. The building later became a smart dwelling. (I.Wright)

GLANYLLYN

112. Space was provided for four tracks, but only the platform ones were laid. This July 1960 view reveals that only the through ones were provided after relaying for coal trains. The goods yard closed with the station on 20th July 1931, following the worst of the depression. (M.Hale)

NANTGARW LOW LEVEL HALT

113.   Both suffixes were added on 1st July 1924. The footpaths and one nameboard remained in September 1957 as evidence of this rail level halt. The track had been removed in October 1940 and had been relaid. (M.Hale)

114.   Leaving Nantgarw Colliery on 30th July 1960 is 0-6-0PT no. 8420. The route closed in April 1987 after the colliery ceased production. This signalbox was opened in June 1952, to control access to the colliery. It was closed in September 1964. (M.Hale)

UPPER BOAT

115.   There had once been a footbridge across the tracks here, but there had been only two lines, not the four allowed for. The date is 30th July 1960. (M.Hale)

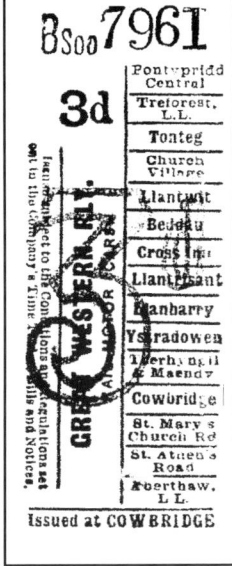

RHYDYFELIN HALT LOW LEVEL

116. The nameboard is just obscured by this CR steam railcar, sometime in 1911. The boarding areas are linked by the foot crossing. This was the terminus for the life of the branch and Rhydyfelin Viaduct was only ever used by a ceremonial train. Low Level was applied from 1924. (A.Dudman coll.)

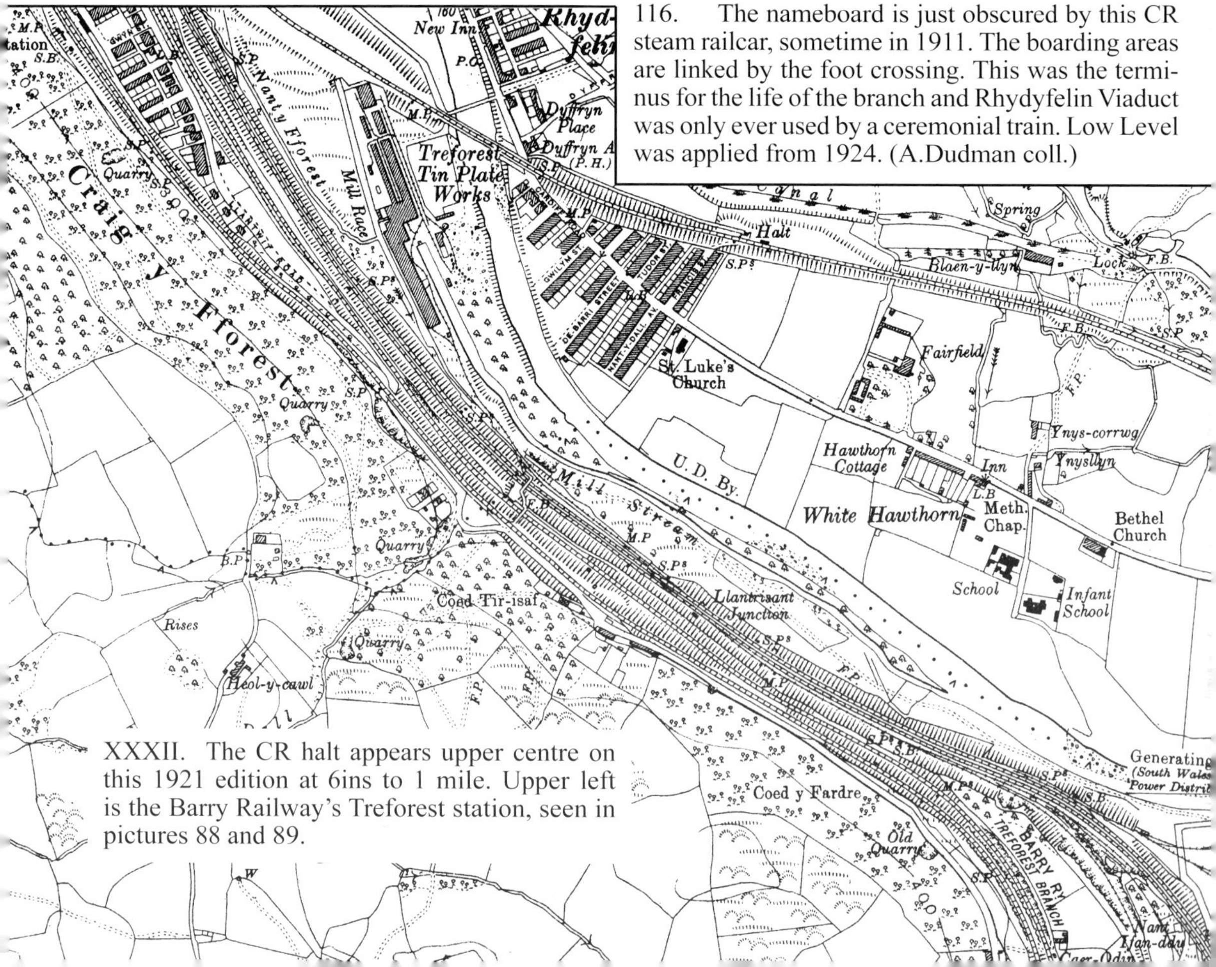

XXXII. The CR halt appears upper centre on this 1921 edition at 6ins to 1 mile. Upper left is the Barry Railway's Treforest station, seen in pictures 88 and 89.

6. To Taff Vale from Ninian Park
NINIAN PARK

117.   Initially called a "Platform" and later termed a "Halt", this stop opened on 2nd November 1912 and was for many years used just by football specials and some weekend trains for seaside visitors. The up platform had been added in 1934 and there were a few regular trains until 1939. For example, in July 1937 there was a 2.29pm to Porthcawl on Sundays. One could return at 8.0pm, the train originating at Newport. In the background is the connection to the main line at Leckwith Junction, which was added in 1932. The view is from the east on 21st April 1962. (M.Hale)

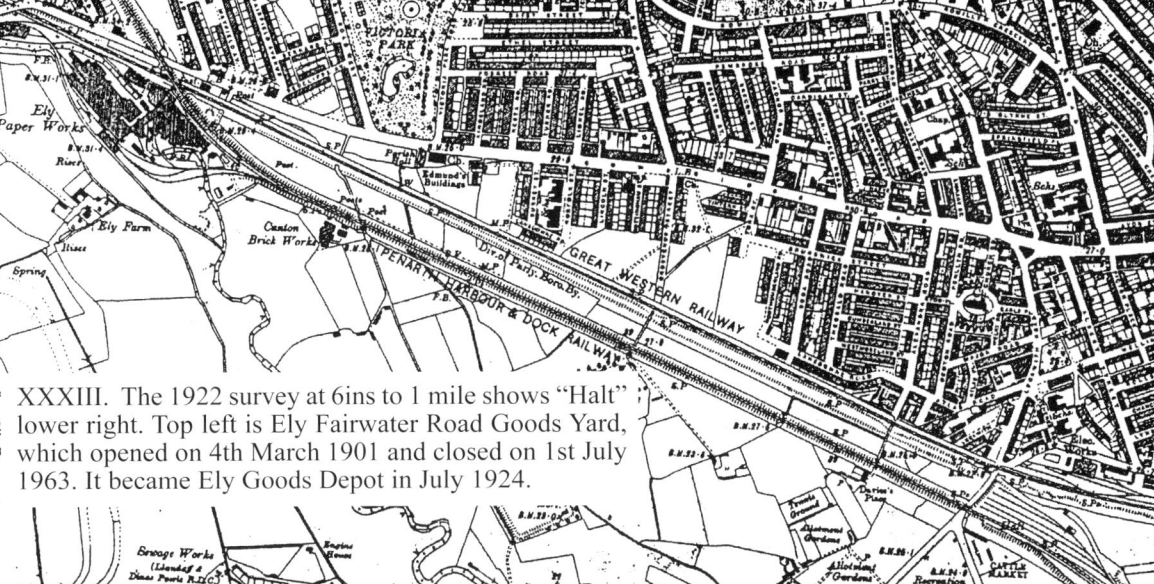

XXXIII. The 1922 survey at 6ins to 1 mile shows "Halt" lower right. Top left is Ely Fairwater Road Goods Yard, which opened on 4th March 1901 and closed on 1st July 1963. It became Ely Goods Depot in July 1924.

118.   We look in the other direction on 20th March 2011 to see the rebuilt station which opened in 1987 for the City Line service. Canton Depot is in the distance. The nearby goods yard closed in April 1966. (D.K.Jones)

CARDIFF and RHYDYFELIN (Motor Cars—One class only).—Great Western (late Cardiff).

Up. — Week Days.

Miles		mrn	mrn	mrn	mrn S		aft	aft	aft		aft	aft	aft	aft	aft		aft	aft	aft	
	Cardiff (Parade)....dep.	5 20	7 0	8 50	1120		1250	1 5	2 35		4 0	5 10	5 35	6 30	7 15		8 30	9 30	1045	
4¼	Whitchurch (Glam.) ¶ ..	5 34	7 14	9 3	1134		1 4	1 18	2 49		4 14	5 23	5 49	6 43	7 29		8 43	9 44	1058	
5¾	Tongwynlais...........	5 41	7 21		1141		1 11		2 56		4 21		5 56		7 36			9 51		
7¾	Glanyllyn ¶	5 47	7 27		1147		1 17		3 2		4 27		6 2		7 42			9 7		
9¼	Upper Boat......[(L.L.)	5 54	7 34		1154		1 24		3 9		4 34		6 9		7 49			10 4		
10¼	Rhydyfelin Halt arr.	5 57	7 37		1157		1 27		3 12		4 37		6 12		7 52			10 7		

Up. — Sundays.

	mrn		mrn		aft		aft		aft		aft		aft		aft	
Cardiff (Parade)........dep.	9 30		1045		1250		1 35		2 30		4 40		6 20		7 50		8 35
Whitchurch (Glam.) ¶ ..	9 43		1058		1 3		1 48		2 44		4 54		6 34		8 3		8 49
Tongwynlais...........									2 52		5 2		6 42				8 57
Glanyllyn ¶									2 58		5 8		6 48				9 3
Upper Boat...........									3 5		5 15		6 55				9 10
Rhydyfelin Halt (L.L.) arr.									3 8		5 18		6 58				9 13

Down. — Week Days.

Miles	Low Level,	mrn	mrn	mrn		aft S	aft	aft	aft	aft		aft	aft	aft	aft	aft		aft	aft	
	Rhydyfelin Halt ..dep.	6 10	7 55			12 5		1 45	3 25	4 45			6 20		8 5			1015		
1	Upper Boat ¶	6 13	7 58			12 8		1 48	3 28	4 48			6 23		8 8			1018		
3¼	Glanyllyn ¶	6 20	8 5			1215		1 55	3 35	4 55			6 30		8 15			1025		
5	Tongwynlais ¶	6 26	8 12			1221		2 1	3 41	5 1			6 36		8 21			1031		
6¾	Whitchurch (Glam.) ¶ ..	6 33	8 20	9 10		1228	1 50	2 10	3 48	5 8		5 45	6 43	7 10	8 28	8 55		1038	11 5	
10¼	Cardiff ** 82 arr.	6 47	8 35	9 24		1242	2 4	2 25	4 2	5 22		5 59	6 57	7 24	8 42	9 9		1052	1119	

Down. — Sundays.

Low Level,	mrn		mrn		aft		aft		aft		aft		aft		aft		aft	
Rhydyfelin Halt ....dep.							3 30		5 30		7 5				9 25		
Upper Boat ¶							3 33		5 33		7 8				9 28		
Glanyllyn							3 40		5 40		7 15				9 35		
Tongwynlais ¶							3 46		5 46		7 21				9 41		
Whitchurch (Glam.) ¶ ..	1020		1110		1 10		2 0	3 53		5 53		7 28		8 10		9 48	
Cardiff ** 82 arr.	1034		1124		1 24		2 14	4 7		6 7		7 42		8 24		10 2	

E Except Saturdays.   S Saturdays only.

¶ "Halts" at Heath (Low Level) and at Rhiwbina, between Cardiff and Whitchurch (Glam.); at Coryton, between Whitchurch (Glam.) and Tongwynlais: and at Nantgarw (Low Level), between Glanyllyn and Upper Boat.
** Parade; about 1 mile to General Station.

July 1924

WAUN-GRON PARK

119.   The new station was recorded on 28th August 1991, as unit no. 150273 works the 15.45 Radyr to Coryton, a U-shaped route. (N.Sprinks)

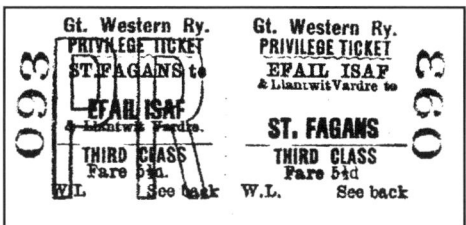

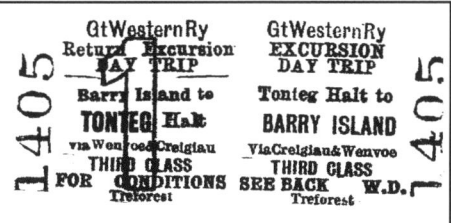

FAIRWATER

120.   The 11.16 Radyr to Coryton was photographed on 8th April 1992, it being worked by Pacer no. 143609. The site of Waterhall Junction is in the background. The mineral line appears on map II, but not the new stations. (N.Sprinks)

CARDIFF and RHYDYFELIN--(Rail Motor Car--One class only).

Up.	Week Days only.
	mrn mrn mrn mrn mrn mrn aft aft aft aft aft aft aft aft aft aft aft aft aft aft
	W W S E S E W S W E W
Miles	
Cardiff (Queen St.) dep.	5 20 7 5 8 10 8 25 8 50 9 50 11 20 12 5 12 40 12 50 1 6 1 25 2 40 3 57 5 14 5 42 6 26 30 7 15 8 42 9 30 10 55
4¼ Whitchurch (Glam.) ¶..	5 35 7 20 8 24 8 39 9 4 10 4 11 35 12 19 12 54 1 51 22 1 40 2 56 4 12 5 30 5 58 6 17 6 44 7 30 8 56 9 45 11 9
5¾ Tongwynlais	5 40 7 25 .. .. .. 11 40 .. .. .. 1 27 .. 3 1 4 17 .. 6 3 .. 7 35 .. 9 51 ..
7¾ Glanylyn ¶	5 45 7 30 .. .. .. 11 45 .. .. .. 1 32 .. 3 6 4 22 .. 6 8 .. 7 40 .. 9 56 ..
9¾ Upper Boat ......(I.L.)	5 51 7 36 .. .. .. 11 51 .. .. .. 1 38 .. 3 12 4 28 .. 6 14 .. 7 46 .. 10 2 ..
10¾ **Rhydyfelin** Halt arr.	5 54 7 39 .. .. .. 11 54 .. .. .. 1 41 .. 3 15 4 31 .. 6 17 .. 7 49 .. 10 5 ..

Down.	Week Days only.
Low Level	mrn mrn mrn mrn mrn aft aft aft aft aft aft aft aft aft aft aft aft aft aft
	W S E S E S W W W W E W W
Miles	
Rhydyfelin Halt...dep.	6 0 7 52 .. .. .. 12 5 .. .. 1 50 3 35 4 40 .. 6 42 7 58 .. 10 10 ..
¾ Upper Boat ¶	6 2 7 54 .. .. .. 12 7 .. .. 1 52 3 37 4 42 .. 6 44 8 0 .. 10 12 ..
3 Glanyllyn	6 7 7 59 .. .. .. 12 12 .. .. 1 57 3 42 4 47 .. 6 49 8 5 .. 10 17 ..
4¼ Tongwynlais ¶......	6 12 8 4 .. .. .. 12 17 .. .. 2 2 3 47 4 52 .. 6 54 8 10 .. 10 22 ..
6¾ Whitchurch (Glam.) ¶..	6 19 8 12 8 32 8 50 9 15 10 13 10 24 12 55 1 30 1 50 2 2 2 11 3 54 5 0 5 45 6 23 6 50 7 5 8 17 9 21 10 29 11 15
10¾ **Cardiff A 52, 55a** .arr.	6 33 8 27 8 46 9 4 9 29 10 27 10 38 1 9 1 44 2 4 2 15 2 25 4 8 5 14 5 59 6 37 7 4 7 19 8 31 9 16 10 43 11 30

A Queen Street; over ⅓ mile to General Station   E Except Saturdays   S Saturdays only.   W Workmen's Train.
¶ **Halts** at Heath (Low Level) at Birchgrove and at Rhiwbina, between Cardiff and Whitchurch (Glam.); at Coryton (Glam.), between Whitchurch (Glam.) and Tongwynlais; and at Nantgarw (Low Level), between Glanyllyn and Upper Boat.

November 1930

DANESCOURT

121.   Nearing retirement age, no. C392 arrives on 28th August 1991, while working the 15.15 Radyr to Coryton service. The provision of City Line/Countryride has done much to reduce road traffic. (N.Sprinks)

122.   The TVR150 special was run on 27th October 1991 from Cardiff Central to Aberdare and it made more history by returning on this route, which has been largely devoid of steam since the steam era. Brighton-built 2-6-4T no. 80080 had a train of five coaches of jubilant admirers. (N.Sprinks)

MP Middleton Press

EVOLVING THE ULTIMATE RAIL ENCYCLOPEDIA

Easebourne Lane, Midhurst, West Sussex.
GU29 9AZ Tel:01730 813169

www.middletonpress.co.uk email:info@middletonpress.co.uk
A-978 0 906520 B- 978 1 873793 C- 978 1 901706 D-978 1 904474 E- 978 1 906008

All titles listed below were in print at time of publication - please check current availability by looking at our website - *www.middletonpress.co.uk* or by requesting a Brochure which includes our *LATEST* RAILWAY TITLES also our TRAMWAY, TROLLEYBUS, MILITARY and WATERWAYS series